Growing Older, Thinking Younger

NIXON

GROWING OLDER,

THINKING YOUNGER

Ministry with Boomers

KEITH A. HAEMMELMANN

THE PILGRIM PRESS
CLEVELAND

THIS BOOK IS DEDICATED TO MY WIFE, JEANNE,
MY CHILDREN, AND THOSE CHURCH MEMBERS
WHO HAVE LOVED AND PATIENTLY SUPPORTED ME
DURING MY THIRTY-PLUS YEARS OF MINISTRY.

The Pilgrim Press, 700 Prospect Avenue, Cleveland, Ohio 44115
thepilgrimpress.com
© 2012 by Keith Haemmelmann

Unless otherwise noted, the Scripture quotations contained herein are from
the New Revised Standard Version Bible, © 1989 by the Division of Christian Education of the National Council of Churches of Christ in the U.S. A.,
and are used by permission. Changes may have been made for inclusivity.

Printed in the United States of America on acid-free paper

16   15   14   13   12   5   4   3   2   1

Library of Congress Cataloging-in-Publication Data

Haemmelmann, Keith, 1956–
    Growing older, thinking younger : ministry with boomers / Keith
Haemmelmann.
      pages cm
    ISBN 978-0-8298-1988-5 (alk. paper)
    1. Church work with the baby boom generation.   2. Church work with
older people—United Church of Christ.   3. Retirement—Religious
aspects—Christianity.   4. Older people—Religious life.   I. Title.
    BV4435.H34 2012
    259'.3—dc23   2012033083.

CONTENTS

INTRODUCTION

I t seems like just yesterday, I was reading *A Generation of Seekers* by
Wade Clark Roof and personally witnessing the growth phenomena
of Saddleback, Willow Creek, and other churches that had targeted
the unchurched, nontraditional, self-focused, anti-institutional
generation labeled Baby Boomers. Twenty-five years later we are
still talking about this generation and their impact upon America.
The discussion, however, no longer revolves around them becoming
parents, but grandparents—not upward mobility, but retirement
stability. And early indications are that this generation, 76.4 million
strong—eight thousand of whom are reaching the age of sixty every
day—will move as dynamically into the final years of their lives as
they did earlier stages.

CNN reports that "the boomer generation will change the way
we think about retirement and aging, just as they transformed notions of relationships—with delayed marriages, fewer children,
more divorces—and ideas about careers, with more women in the
workplace and adult learning."[1] Everything I observe within my
church indicates that this transition is occurring quickly, and we
either embrace this demographic shift as an opportunity for re-
newed ministry, or we miss it.

I was startled awake to this transition when, in one year, I
conducted nearly forty memorial services out of a congregational
membership of one thousand individuals. A shocking number even
by Florida standards! As one might expect, the majority of these
memorials involved individuals from the last stages of the "G.I.

generation" (1901–1924) and earlier years of the "silent generation" (1925–1945), not a totally unanticipated progression, but one that woke me from a complacency regarding my church and its future. Shocking, especially since I have always prided myself on a ministry that tried to emphasize *vision and growth*! But what I had missed, or inappropriately assumed, was that growth took place on the youthful end of the demographic spectrum and that by, I guess, the natural order of things, the older constituency would just always be there. Why? Because they always had been. But before my eyes, I was witnessing the very opposite. A lot of familiar faces were no longer present. There were gaps in the pews. Gifts missing from our offerings. These were all changes that I intuitively knew were coming but had not prepared for, at least not in any intentional way. It was suddenly clear: our congregation rested on the precipice of what could become a rather quick downward spiral, unless some things changed. And never one to "go down without a fight," I vowed that things would change . . . and they did!

How? Well, we began by examining the demographics of our community. We knew that the residents of St. Pete Beach were predominately retirees, had been for years, and things had moved along just fine. Why weren't the new retirees simply coming to church, replacing the previous ones, as they always had? Something had to be going on, but what was it? What we discovered was that, yes, we were still surrounded by retirees or soon-to-be retirees, but these retirees were different—motivated by a different set of values and driven by a whole new list of goals and visions. These retirees were Baby Boomers. And with these Boomers came a contrasting approach to beach life, worship life, and all things in general to do with life.

We always knew they were coming; we'd talked about them for years! Still, we had been caught without a strategy for this transition, assuming that what had always worked for attracting retirees would simply continue to work. What our church came to be aware of was that, as with every stage of their lives, Boomers were approaching this phase (retirement) differently than their predecessors, and what had worked previously would probably not work again. Now, it would be easy to write my experience off as particular to settings like Florida or Arizona, but I don't believe this is the case. The percentages may vary from location to location, but the challenge of this generational transition is the same everywhere. And our churches either acknowledge and address the unique characteristics of this generation or miss the opportunity it presents.

What is of concern is that clergy I contacted in the course of this writing are fully aware of the demographic tsunami headed their way, but few are doing anything to intentionally target the specific needs or unique characteristics of Boomers. In most cases their churches are successful, but from a model designed for generations currently retired. When asked to name a specific area of ministry or one program that appeals to those between the ages of forty-six and sixty-five, more times than not the response was silence. This says to me that we have a generational gap in our vision for the church's future along with holes in our current ministries. We are as unprepared for Boomers at this stage of their lives as we were when they passed through earlier stages in their lives. So what will happen when those currently retired are gone? Who will take the place of those generations that have been the stalwarts of our congregations?

If there's any consolation, churches are not alone in being ill-prepared for this wave of Boomers moving toward retirement. Matilda White Riley, a noted gerontologist, sees a significant "structural lag" in many of the arenas supposedly "in touch" with the needs of those in or about to enter retirement, whether traditional living communities, health-care programs, or volunteer organizations.[2] An article in the January 16, 2012, *USA Today* illustrates this shift as golf communities, once the "gold standard" for retirement, find themselves struggling to maintain their magnetism. Fewer Boomers are playing the game, instead seeking other forms of recreation and community in their end years.[3]

Riley attributes this "gap" in our thinking to what she identifies as misunderstanding "the capacity and interests" of aging Boomers. "We face a burgeoning mismatch between demographics and opportunities, and the demographics are way ahead."[4] Boomers don't want to just "keep busy" in retirement, they want to be significantly involved. They desire purpose; they want to make a difference; and, even after full lives, they are still on a quest for *meaning* in life. They are not seeking to be disengaged in their anticipated years of retirement, as Webster's dictionary would lead us to believe, but reengaged in this yet-to-be redefined phase of life. In summation, their desire is to finish strong! Thus they do not view their final stage of living as one of "vegetation and recreation," in Daniel Boostin's words, but of "creation" and re-creation.[5] So Riley arrives at the same conclusion that I have, that is, we think we are prepared for this generation but are "missing the boat," and unless we shed some of our long-held assumptions about retirement and those entering it, we will be out of sync. And for the church this means missing this generation, once again.

Ralph Waldo Emerson once wrote, "Every wall is a door." Many congregations are rapidly approaching that "wall." Proof can be found in the increasing number of churches that are permanently closing their doors, every day. As I gazed out over my congregation from my vantage point in the pulpit and looked on all the faces that had been present in, now absent from, my congregation, I realized that if the course of our church ministry did not change, that would be our destination as well. Not quickly, but eventually. We could run from the demographics shifting around us, but we most certainly could not hide. Things were about to change, and quickly. We needed to change too! So, what to do? How could we turn our wall into a door?

In a small way, that is the intent of this book—to gain a quick look into this Boomer generation with all of its subtle complexities, idiosyncrasies, and variable twists. We must accept that they are different and that, to engage them in our church's work and ministry, we must become different too. America *is* aging, and our churches are aging along with it. This could be viewed as a pattern for despair, but I would choose to see it as an occasion for great hope. For the irony of all this is, as America grows older, our churches have the opportunity of becoming younger—focusing on the Boomers coming our way. The challenge for ministry is to recognize this generation's uniqueness, identifying the means by which to meet their needs, find focus for their energy, fulfill their drive for purpose, while spiritually enabling them to grow. It is a very big task, but an incredibly wonderful challenge! Mark Twain, in his usual witty way, shares a meaningful insight taken from his days working on the Mississippi: "Two things seemed pretty apparent to me. One was, that in order to be a (Mississippi River) pilot a man had got to learn more than any one man ought to be allowed to know; and the other was that he must learn it all over again in a different way every 24 hours."[6]

It is time to "learn it all over again in a different way," navigating our church's future based upon Boomers and what they bring with them as they sail toward retirement. My church has begun to set this new course for its future with positive results. In some small way, I hope this book provides a compass for your congregation to do the same.

1

A STARBUCKS EPIPHANY

A key tenet of my denomination, the United Church of Christ, is "God Is Still Speaking." I couldn't have experienced this expression more clearly than when I stood in line at Starbucks, waiting for my morning jolt of java. There, within that sacred space where Boomers pause to meditate, congregate, and daily associate, I found myself staring at the community bulletin board displayed behind one of the counters (that there is a "community" board already says something). There, posted from top to bottom and side to side, were invitations to seminars on "Spiritual Engineering" and Buddhism; the schedule for this weekend's "Walk-Run" to fight breast cancer; notices of Sunday's Sunset Drum Circle on the beach; a Wednesday night presentation on health care; and a Friday evening program of soulful music and poetry. Oh, and did I mention the upcoming book signing?

Truly, I could stop writing here, for anyone with the slightest desire to gain insight into current culture, especially regarding Boomers, could do so by stopping to look—really look—at a similar bulletin board, as I did that one in Starbucks. Yet, in all honesty, I had walked by that "signpost" a hundred times and not given it a second thought! Maybe my blindness was simply a matter of early morning oblivion—I don't wake up easily. Perhaps it was the result of my intense desire to get caffeine in my system. Or maybe it was because I just hadn't been paying attention.

Relevant ministry stands at the junction of life and faith, the crossroad between who we are and what we believe. The role of church leaders is to recognize and identify these points of intersection and interpret what they mean. I had missed what should have been one of the most obvious windows into the Boomer generation—*that bulletin board in Starbucks.* Posted there were clues to Boomers' needs, interests, and passions. And around those "mission statements" in that space, people met, talked, and created community. How could I have not put two and two together? This was my generation. I am . . . them! Ironically, maybe that's why I had missed it. I was living it, so I wasn't objectively analyzing what made my peers tick, what we are about.

In that moment, lightning struck and God spoke, as I realized the considerable time and energy I had focused on maintaining continuity for older generations of my congregation while believing the "generational jump" I needed to make in ministry was toward those in their twenties and thirties. And don't misunderstand, we must care for and reach people at both ends of the age spectrum. But in my "Aha" moment, staring at that bulletin board, waiting for my wife's "no fat, no foam, extra hot, vanilla latte," I realized what I had overlooked—ignored, missed—the immediate bridge to the church's future, the "pearl of great value" (Matt. 13:46)—my own generation. *Boomers!* Wow! An epiphany, right there, in a corner of Starbucks. It was time to rethink and reshape my ministry, and maybe you should yours, as well.

It was then that I decided to investigate the explicit and implicit clues to this generation as revealed by this bulletin board, in order to discern what they meant for the future focus of the congregation I served. Still, I couldn't help but think how ironic, after all, that I had spent the majority of my pastoral career serving churches loaded with Boomers, yet I really hadn't given them the intentionality that their numbers and presence deserved. Like most churches, mine had provided a wide variety of programs primarily aimed at meeting their needs through ministries directed toward their children (preschools, after-school arts and music programs, youth groups, and the like). But what about them individually? Personally? And what would happen to them, in relation to the church, when their children were grown and gone?

I suspect that this oversight was due, at least in part, to the fact that leadership within most churches I have served stemmed foremost from members in their fifties and up. That was where the commitment and concurrent funding lay; therefore, that was the age group with whom my time and energy was most invested. But guess what, that age group was now us—me, Boomers—and Boomers have always sought to be, and to do, things differently. Thus they cannot be assumed to automatically fill our pews or leadership roles as they grow older. And where they do, it will certainly not be in the same way or with the same expectations as previous generations. Church leaders either wake up to this generational shift that is occurring, or congregations will continue down the slippery slope of decline. I was stunned to learn, while recently attending a gathering of ministers in the United Church of Christ, that, in terms of age of congregants, we are now the oldest mainline denomination in the United States. Obviously something has been transpiring that needs to be identified and targeted with subsequent changes, not for the sake of mere numbers or the salvation of any one denomination, but for the purpose of reaching and retaining, not "the greatest generation," but the largest generation, my own.

My inquiry into what this "generational thing" might be about began by my inviting a number of Boomers to my house for a casual night of open discussion around questions, such as these:

- How do you view the church, at this point in your life?
- Where does the church intersect your "day-to-day"?
- What does faith mean to you?
- What opportunities do you see for the church to better minister to you and your peers?
- What do you see as the future of retirement?
- Is there anything different that you hope for at this stage in your life than maybe your parents did?
- In a word or short phrase, how would you describe how you wish to finish your life?

The insights gained from these conversations were enlightening and insightful, as I began to realize that Boomers were not simply moving toward retirement, they were intent upon "redefining it." They were, as Phyllis Moen points out in her article "Midcourse: Navigating Retirement and a New Life Stage," actually creating a new phase in our perception of aging as they disengaged from their previous responsibilities of career and child raising and sought to be differently engaged, rather than unengaged in the latter stages of their lives.[1]

It became immediately apparent that potluck suppers and travelog luncheons were not going to capture the attention and retain the interest of Boomers. Retirement for them meant the time and energy to do new and perhaps better things, to contribute to life in ways no longer dictated by work schedules or social obligations. Sure, there were family responsibilities of a different nature, but also a new-found freedom to redefine who you were and the way you would experience the final stage of life. For them, this final stage of life was not about a rocking chair, but a rocket ship that would take them on their last great adventure. It meant finishing strong, leaving a creative and lasting legacy, concluding a life's story not with a period but with an exclamation mark! So what were their responses to my questions? Here are just a few.

WHAT ARE YOUR VIEWS AND EXPECTATIONS OF RETIREMENT?

- I feel like a kid in a candy store. I have time to do anything I want—but then you realize you have no time because you became so involved.

- I love retirement, but it seems like I'm busier than I ever was before. There are so many opportunities to do things and everyone wants me to do *their* thing. It's hard to discern what I should do . . . what I'm called to do.

- I want to be a part of "the body of Christ." But what I love about our church is that it acknowledges and encourages my individual journey as well.

- Since I've retired, I love pursuing all the opportunities for learning—passions that I've had all my life. It's just that, now, I have the time to pursue them. We did a field trip with a seeing-eye dog, the other day. It was fascinating.

- After working in a corporation, under management, I love the opportunity to figure out for myself what to do, when, and where.

- I was planning on retiring five years ago, but now, I do not want to retire—I *want* to keep on working. I guess what I am looking for is work, but with flexibility.

- My biggest concerns are about health—ten years from now, will I be able to do what I want to do? That is why we planned the aggressive, more physical trips and activities early in our retirement.

- I don't see retirement as a destination, but as a turning season in my life.

- I hate the word "retirement." This is just a "mid-life" transition.

- The last year and a half our business has been challenging. We don't know if the business will survive. Learning to turn it over to God. What this has taught me is that there is a side to life other than work! My husband and I are learning the beauty of new living.

- The word retirement either disappears in the future or will be drastically different. Our generation broke down barriers. We believed the possibilities were limitless. Why would we think differently about retirement?

- We didn't have children until our mid to late thirties. I have to work into my seventies.

- Why retire? Activities that would have been in retirement are coming into my life now, just as my work will somehow extend into whatever my years of "retirement" are. *The borders* (such as mandatory retirement at sixty-five) *are becoming blurred* or totally disappearing.

- We're sandwiched between care of our children and the care of our parents. All our "time off" is spent visiting either my parents or my husband's parents.
- I want to work, but with less stress. It's not about the money. It's not about the Wall Street retirement figures anymore. What the last few years have taught me is, I can live, and live well in the best sense, with whatever money I have.

WHY DON'T YOUR FRIENDS COME TO CHURCH?

- Think they can do it on their own, but they miss community. I wonder how they will make it when their health fails or death hits home.
- Religion is a damaged brand in the Western world.
- They say they're spiritual, but not necessarily religious. But what I don't see is how they live that spiritual identity out.
- I've never looked to the church to give me direction in life, but to keep me from derailing on my journey.
- I got married on the beach, which surprised my friends because *I so loved the church*—but for me, the gazebo on the beach *was* the church—God's church, God's sanctuary.
- Time! It's all about "not enough time"!
- Over the last several years, I have actually seen them become more spiritual, if not religious. Before, if I asked team members if they wanted to pray before staff meetings—and I work at hospice—they would stutter and resist. Now, they bow their heads and I think, "Wow!"

WHAT DO YOU WANT FROM THE CHURCH?

- I attended a church where, during their worship announcements, a young adult—I believe a teacher—stood up and spoke about the needs of a teenager—intelligent and motivated, but without family or home. I came to discover that the congregation adopted that teen "as their own." They purchased clothing, provided assistance to the family that took him in, and created a college fund. Now that's the community of faith that inspires me. That's the kind of place to which I want to belong.

- It's critical that the church helps us to take care of each other.
- I want the church to challenge me, throw down the gauntlet; call me to do something different, keep me evolving.
- Provide the motivation required to change my life—change the world.
- More intimate, small groups, where I can explore my faith and spiritually grow.
- I want the church to make the gospel relevant for *my* life. I want the church to be real, not ritualistic.
- I look to older members in the church as role models for my life and I want to become a role model for those following me.
- What I've discovered at this point in life is how much the *learning* part of my church life means.
- I want the church to help me define who I am and who I wish to become at this stage in my life.
- I got involved in church to make sense out of my life. Now, it's all about relationships.
- Church provides for me not just religious friendships, but family friendships. I have no family nearby. We're not close anyway. But every time I go to church, it's like a family reunion.
- I love the "Still Speaking Daily Devotional" (www.ucc.org). I read it every day; it provides a daily "call to action" for me.
- I was on my way to work, listening to talk radio when the announcer took off on a tirade about belonging to his church, *the church of IDM, it don't matter!* "It don't matter what you wear. It don't matter what you do! It don't matter how you

act! It don't matter what you believe! It just don't matter!
That's my church!" It was then that it struck me—it does
matter—and I need a place to figure out what that means!

- At this stage, I would break life into five categories—the
melding of a lot of things with different levels of intensity.
  1. A need for community.
  2. Support on my individual journey.
  3. Support in my spiritual journey. Help in becoming more
  spiritually aware, engaged, open minded, body, soul . . .
  "something *other*."
  4. A presence in my moral journey (though I don't really need
  the church for this); I have a lot of scientific friends who are
  not religious, but very good, and, I think, moral people.
  5. Development of my faith journey. How it all fits together.
  More analytical.

These comments were not altogether surprising. What was surprising is that within all the dreams, aspirations, and concerns
shared, few participants had any kind of plan as to how they were
going to navigate into retirement. They were "just going to figure
it out." I believe this may provide an "opening" for the church to
connect with and assist this generation as they reassess their spirituality and its implications for this last phase of life. How *are* they
going to spend their time? Their resources? What will be of value
to them now that they have the flexibility and autonomy to determine those things? But to accomplish this, churches must revisit
their perception of ministry to those entering retirement. This begins by better understanding this unique generation.

Before proceeding, I must confess that I had never considered
isolating this generation so that our church could specifically address their unique needs in our planning. However, just as I would
never consider implementing a program designed for teenagers
with elementary school children, or programs created around the

specific needs of men, for women—or vice versa—why would I "lump" all retirees together? Hmmm. I guess I saw them as, well, simply retirees. But this is neither accurate, nor will it be effective in the years ahead. We need to look at all areas of our ministry, generation to generation. And in this instance, the area of ministry is retirement and the generation to consider is the largest our country has ever known. Baby Boomers! What a blessed challenge to have.

"Grandpa, explain again how you stopped the Vietnam war by growing a beard and picking flowers."

77.3 MILLION BOOMERS

PART ONE

What Makes Boomers Tick? Boomers Are . . .

REFLECTING ON CONVERSATIONS as well as the thoughts of those who have studied this generation, I see a number of consistent themes, or characteristics, coalescing that can be associated with Boomers. Some of these may resonate with you immediately; they did with me! That is, I intuitively recognized some behaviors that could be linked to this generation. What was altered by this more in-depth evaluation was their clarification. By categorizing and naming certain characteristics, I could begin to "wrap my mind" around them, thus beginning to formulate specific elements that needed to be included/addressed in the formation of our church's programming.

But before proceeding, let's set aside some of the assumptions and stereotypes we may carry regarding aging, retirement, and the final stages of life, such as these:

- Growing old is, well, growing old—forming one large homogenous group that is the same for every generation.
- Becoming a senior citizen automatically means choosing rest and recreation over engaged and active living.
- Retirement means "stepping aside," "winding down," becoming more passive.
- It means accepting that your best years are behind you.
- "You can't teach an 'old dog' new tricks."

Adjusting these preconceived notions of retirement is the first step toward renegotiating our goal of designing ministries that meet the specific needs and ideals of this generation.

So, who are these Boomers? What motivates them, defines them, and makes them tick?

2

PHYSICALLY ACTIVE AND
DETERMINED TO STAY THAT WAY

This Boomer characteristic is revealed in the numerous sanctuaries dedicated to the achievement and maintenance of physical health. These chapels and cathedrals can be found in the form of community centers, private health clubs, and the inclusion of designated rooms, or even floors, in downtown hotels as well as corporate office buildings. The shaman is a personal exercise trainer and the bible an organic protein food menu. This Boomer characteristic may stem from the emphasis on physical exercise initiated in the early stages of their childhood development, during the influential years of the Kennedy administration. Then again, it may simply be the result of the ever increasing awareness of personal health over their lifespan. In any case, exercise/health/activity are intrinsic to the DNA of this generation.

"Boomers are the first generation that grew up exercising, and the first that expects, indeed demands, that they be able to exercise into their '70's," said Dr. Nicholas A. DiNubile, a Philadelphia-area orthopedic surgeon, who coined and trademarked the term 'boomeritis.'"[1]

In 1999, the International Health, Racket, and Sports Association set a ten-year goal of doubling its membership from fifty million to a hundred million. Interestingly enough, by 2006 the association had not only achieved but exceeded that goal, resetting it for 120 million.[2] Who were the greatest single group that contributed to this growth? Baby Boomers.

Linked closely to this desire to remain physically active is the Boomer objective of remaining socially active and engaged as well. A quick look around reveals that Boomers have no intention of "riding into the sunset" as they age, but rather plan to continue putting their imaginations and talents to work in ways that will have an ongoing cultural impact. An illustration of this occurred when Boomer Bill Cowher resigned as head coach of the Pittsburgh Steelers. During his announcement he purposely avoided using the word "retirement," saying, "That [word] makes you feel old." So instead of becoming "retired," he chose a course that enabled him to be "re-hired," finding work and purpose in a new way as a sports broadcast analyst.[3]

Another example of this desire to remain on the center stage of society is the ongoing presence of rock stars who continue to actively tour into their "golden" years: AC/DC lead singer Brian Johnson, age sixty-three; Eagles singer Glenn Frey, age sixty-two; Aerosmith's Steven Tyler, sixty-one; James Taylor, age sixty-two. It was "rocker" Tom Petty, sixty-one, who once crooned, "I don't know, but I've been told, you never slow down, you never grow old."[4] Indications are, for Boomers, these words still carry deep meaning.

As I reflected on this characteristic and its impact upon my congregation over the last eight years, it dawned on me that one reason we struggle, especially in regard to the sedentary nature of committees and meetings, is that Boomers do not want to serve in these capacities. And it's not because they don't want to lead or be in an atmosphere where they can express their ideas, but given the choice between sitting in a meeting or actively, physically doing something, they will choose the latter every time. The most successful committees in my congregation are literally the most active (physically) committees. That is, their decisions lead them to clear and specific, hands-on forms of response. And who make up the majority sitting on those boards? Boomers!

Bottom line? Boomers want to remain healthy so they can continue being personally active and socially significant. They hope to retire from work, but not necessarily the public scene. Rather, as they move toward the later stages of their lives, they wish to pursue new passions and engage in purposeful endeavors they feel matter—efforts that clearly contribute not just to their spiritual, but also their physical, well-being. "Which commandment is the most important of all?" Jesus was once asked. To which he replied, "Love God with all your heart, your soul, your strength, and your mind" (Luke 10:27–28 RSV). In reference to Boomers, you can't be more on target than that![5]

3

Enchanted by Youth

s that Rod Stewart I hear humming "forever young" in the back of my mind? Hand in hand with their expectations for good health and an active lifestyle is the Boomer desire to remain youthful in thinking, attitude, and wherever possible, physical appearance. This characteristic is so dominant that some professionals refer to it as "psychological neoteny" (Greek *neos*, for "young," and *teinein*, "to extend").[1] Evidence of this self-perception can be heard in expressions such as "Age is only in your head" and "Fifty is the new forty." According to a 2009 Pew Research survey, the typical Boomer believes that old age doesn't begin until age seventy-two.[2] J. Walker Smith refers to this attitude as "middle age-lessness," summarizing it best when he writes, "Boomers . . . don't want to live longer as old people; they want to live endlessly as middle-aged people."[3]

The marketplace reflects this "youthful longing" with a production boom in everything from vitamins, oils, and organic foods and skin care products to the dozens of self-help books with titles ranging from *The Ultimate Plan for Reversing the Aging Process* to *The Methuselah Manual: The 3% Secret for Staying Young, Healthy, and Sexy*. Mindful of this characteristic, advertising agencies flood the market with commercials that make you wonder whether you are really watching a sporting event or a repeatedly interrupted Viagra commercial.

If the desired physical look cannot be achieved through Tai Bo, Pilates, or basic health care, Boomers are known to seek the next available option, cosmetic surgery. According to ABC News, the number of cosmetic procedures between 1997 and 2010 rose from 115,709 to 684,768.[4] The American Society of Plastic Surgeons reports that, in 2010, 13.1 million cosmetic procedures were performed in the United States, constituting a 77 percent increase over the previous decade.[5] Certainly, these figures are not exclusive to Boomers; however, the majority are a result of this generation aging. In 1513, Ponce DeLeon searched for the Fountain of Youth in what is now St. Augustine, Florida, and didn't find it. He should have waited until 2011 and visited South Beach instead. He would have been far more successful.

What does this mean? It means that Boomers tend to disassociate themselves from what looks, feels, or appears to be a result of aging—real or not. All of this translates into an aversion to traditional programs, activities, and events that in the past have been the accepted model for moving into the final phase of living.

"Many things have been posited as characteristic of this generation: individualistic, spiritual, organic, experiential, experimental, adventurous, discriminating, extravagant, vigorous, self-righteous, rebellious, skeptical questioning, searching, self-absorbed, self-seeking. To a greater or lesser extent, all of these are true . . . but an underlying mindset of youthfulness accounts for all of them."[6]

4

EXPERIENTIAL: ADVENTURE ORIENTED

Based on the previously identified characteristics of this generation, is it any surprise that Boomers want to do things that are out of the ordinary, adventurous in nature? Their desire is to engage the world around them, experiencing life on multiple levels. One need look no farther than television trends to find a reflection of this attribute as shows like "The Amazing Race" and "Survivor" have increased in popularity over the last ten years while decades-long favorites such as "All My Children" have met their demise. It is not enough for Boomers to simply body surf at Newport Beach, they want to kite surf the Red Sea and windsurf in the Columbia River Gorge. For Boomers, life has always been about "what's around the corner"—"the next great adventure." It's not enough to read about some far-off land, they want to go there. They are not satisfied with flying in an airplane, they would build it, pilot it, and then dare to jump out of it.[1]

This was very apparent in my personal conversation with Boomers as they described the differences between themselves and their parents, summed up by this survey respondent:

> Mom and Dad were children of the Depression. They preserved—they kept—they held things—they waited for the next shoe to drop. You never know when something serious could happen and you might lose it all. They missed so much because they lived by "Murphy's Law." Not me!
>
> Travel? Why do that? Fly? The plane might crash. Visit a foreign land? Things happen in others countries. I

don't believe that Boomers see life like that. At least, I don't, and my parents certainly did. I want to go, see, live, experience other people and places. If something happens, then . . . so be it.

This means that when it comes to "helping others," Boomers do not wish to just feed the hungry, house the homeless, or educate children; they want to personally meet them, speak with them, distribute the food, shingle the roof, and travel to Timbuktu, if necessary, to do so. Statistics show that eighteen million Boomers (25 percent) are willing to volunteer their time for a good cause and 70 percent feel they have a responsibility to make the world a better place, wherever that might take them.[2] In fact, Boomers represent the highest volunteer rate of any generation in America.[3] What an incredible wealth of potential!

An illustration of this in my church occurred when three hundred or so meals were prepared and distributed to the homeless in our city. Nearly two to three times as many people volunteered to serve the food to the homeless as jumped at the opportunity to prepare it. It didn't matter that the shelter was in a "rougher" part of the city or that distributing the food required more time; these volunteers' search for involvement and satisfaction meant direct engagement. In fact, the unfamiliarity of the shelter itself may have been part of the appeal.

No wonder "voluntourism," the combination of travel and overseas mission, is one of the "hottest" new forms of world travel appealing to Boomers. "We travel a fair amount," says Warren, a Hawaiian physician, "but it's valuable to feel connected with other communities . . . beyond seeing tourist sites. It's understanding what we all have in common and . . . seeing the bigger picture." He, along with his family, spent two weeks over Christmas at a refuge for troubled boys near Guatemala City. "It was very rewarding and actually one of the most enjoyable vacations we've ever had, he adds."[4]

In 2006 VolunteerMatch, "the Web's largest volunteer engagement network," commissioned an extensive study, determining that

"Boomers are far more interested in volunteering than they're given credit for." In fact, more than half of adults fifty-five and older who participated in the survey were interested in volunteering. "The challenge is in finding the right opportunity to match their skills and experience."[5] Boomers have never been much about others telling them what to do or think or how to behave. Rather, they have always wanted to see and experience things for themselves.

This is 180 degrees from the forms of ministry offered to older/retired adults by the church when I entered pastoral ministry thirty years ago. Then, involvement centered around attending presentations made by missionaries or those doing ministry on the church's behalf. If you were a member with longevity, eventually you'd be invited to serve on those boards that managed the funds or even designated them for specific ministries. If you wanted to physically participate, then you worked at the annual rummage sale or made cupcakes for the seasonal bake sale, all of which were aimed at raising monies to support the ministries that others— sometimes young adults, at other times foreign missionaries—performed. But the focus or driving force behind these activities seemed to center on what members did within, rather than outside, the church's walls, with satisfaction being derived from the total amount of money raised for various programs or outside missions that other groups or institutions provided.

For Boomers, however, this entire scheme is reversed. It isn't that they don't participate in similar sorts of fellowship-based activities, as they tend to be very relational; it's just that for them the fellowship comes at the end of running a 5K that raises monies to fight breast cancer, or in a beer toast at the conclusion of a week-long mission trip to hurricane-torn New Orleans. It's not that they won't lend their leadership skills to decision-making groups and processes; it's just that their energy is more about the outcomes than the processes. This became very evident as one evening I sat in on a meeting of our church's mission committee—probably the most active committee in my current church. The meeting was brimming with enthusiasm and excitement. Those in attendance were clearly invested in what was transpiring. But they were not simply moving through an agenda, they were developing a strategy and plan for action. As the meeting progressed, it became quite obvious that the synergy came, not from the focus *for* that hour, but the focus *of* that hour—the opportunity to meet, greet, and directly assist those in need. And as I looked around that room, trying to understand what was happening, what was different, I suddenly realized that fourteen of the sixteen people involved were Boomers, and the two who weren't were children of Boomers.

Meetings of this committee weren't like this just a few years ago. A demographic shift had taken place, and with it, the way that ministry functioned. Where once they met to determine how the monthly missions receipts would be allocated, now they converged to put in place next month's plan to directly attack homelessness, hunger, and so on in their backyard as well as elsewhere in the country or world. Tornados in Missouri. What materials can we immediately collect and what's the quickest means of getting them there? Hurricane in Haiti? Who wants to go?

If the church is to reach this generation, it is imperative we rethink what it means to be an "active" (literally) church member. Boomers do not wish to "sit in church" or simply "go to church," but rather want to "be the church"; they do not want their faith journey to end with hearing about Christ, but instead wish to be Christ for their neighbor. Mission is a strong verb, not a generic noun. How challenging and exciting is that?

5

Driven by Passion, Purpose, and Potential

Born into the post–World War II environment of American expansion and prosperity, Boomers didn't so much aspire to the "American Dream," as their parents had; they felt born into it. This created a twofold atmosphere, the first being a belief in *limitless possibility*. Raised in a society that was racing toward the moon, they matured with the notion that they could accomplish anything and life could only get better. Like the NASA astronauts, their motto was "The sky is NOT the limit." The second result of their environment was that, unlike previous generations whose main concern regarded day-to-day living, prosperity freed them to pursue more *self-focused questions,* such as "How do I achieve inner fulfillment?" and "What is the meaning of life?" Thus their national anthem became John Lennon's "Imagine." And their ultimate creation? The personal computer, an invention aimed at empowering the individual beyond what most people could ever have dreamed, giving birth to succession of smaller, quicker, even more empowering personal and portable "I" devices, such as the iPod, iPhone, and iPad, all of which have had a world-altering impact.

Raised in a time shaped by such visionaries and social entrepreneurs as John and Robert Kennedy, as well as Martin Luther King Jr., is it any wonder this generation sought a better world? More importantly, they believed they could make it happen, producing the likes of geniuses such as Bill Gates and Steve Jobs. This is poignantly illustrated in Walter Isaacson's biography *Steve Jobs*, where Jobs attempts to lure John Sculley, an executive at the time with Pepsi, into accepting the position of CEO at Apple:

> Steve's head dropped as he stared at his feet. After a weighty, uncomfortable pause, he issued a challenge that would haunt me for days. "Do you want to spend the rest of your life selling sugared water, or do you want a chance to change the world?"[1]

In part, this characteristic may also explain the tremendous success of Rev. Rick Warren's bestselling book *The Purpose Driven Life,* a text built around such Boomers' questions as "What on earth am I here for?" "What am I called to do?" and "What does God have to do with me?" Boomers want to believe they are here for a specific purpose—their purpose. Perhaps God's purpose. They have always been "seekers." And I strongly suspect that as they age and gain awareness that their time on earth is growing shorter, this attribute will only grow stronger.

A very positive reflection of what this passion can accomplish was witnessed during "Mission 1," an outreach initiative launched by the national offices of the United Church of Christ. The goal was simple but profound—to unite all the congregations in the denomination for eleven days (November 1–11, 2011) to do something about the issue of hunger in America.

- Give eleven dollars!
- Bring eleven food items to church!
- Recruit eleven friends to work at a food kitchen!

In other words: Pull together! Make a dent! Change the world! The effort not only raised money and gathered incredible amounts of food, it achieved something far greater. It motivated people, inspired innovation, and called people to "don't stop believin.'"[2] Boomers in our church loved it!

I can't help but recall a story told by Dean Kelly in the book *Why Fundamentalist Churches Are Growing.* In it he tells of a Methodist minister who learned that an outstanding teenager in his congregation was leaving to join a fundamentalist church. Her reason for doing so (and this person would now be approximately fifty-six years old) was not only concise, but prophetic: "If only you believed what you believe as strongly as they believe what they believe."[3]

Are we passionate about our congregation's ministry? Are we passionate about the role of the church and its future? Do we believe that what we are doing matters? Are we providing just time filler for folks, or offering programs for passionate, personal involvement? If the latter, great! If not, well . . . ?

6

POLITICALLY ACTIVE — SORT OF!

Contrary to what most have been persuaded to believe by events and films such as *Woodstock,* when it comes to politics, Boomers are more like the "Silent generation" that preceded them than not, with a growing number referring to themselves as "conservatives."[1] This proved to be a personal eye-opener when I moved from Colorado to serve a suburban church in Chicagoland that was composed primarily of Boomers. I had made the assumption that they would be progressive, like myself. What I discovered was that, yes, they wanted to impact the world, but often within the matrix of a life modeled by Ward and June Cleaver.

In other words, their core value was "family" and whatever preserved, protected, and promoted *their* family needs. This led to political positions that were often across the board, bound by one common thread—their household. Like so many facets of Boomers' lives, their social concerns were fashioned around their personal lives. Hence, the sociopolitical commitment of Boomers might best be labeled as "tailored engagement."

Boomers will be noticeably absent from a political event in which there is no discussion of issues that clearly affect them. They will be the last to support a candidate because of party affiliation, or only because of a general sense that he or she would make a good legislator. Tailored engagement means that political participation by Boomers will be more like the social engagement of their youth—socially active but skeptical about politics; concerned with their communities or other things that directly affect them; result oriented with more regard for producing benefits than for achieving higher goals or fulfilling moral imperatives; and conducted through arrangements that may neglect the traditional political structures to which their parents felt an allegiance.[2]

This sounds counterintuitive when first placed beside the previously identified characteristic of "passionate," but not really. How can this be? Well, Boomers are often socially liberal but economically conservative. They want to help others, but directly, which often translates into "no" government interference or involvement. Values are important—but to be self-determined. As such, Boomers commit, vote, and invest most in those things that strike "close to home," which also explains why they rally strongly around such causes as breast cancer but are more splintered on such matters as same-gender marriage.[3]

Whether for or against something, Boomers' passion often correlates with how they see it impacting their homes and their pocketbooks. This means that when the cause is "nondebatable," such as hunger, they can be an incredibly powerful force, but when it is more divisive (such as whether gay marriage supports or threatens the family), they can be extremely polarized. In both cases, however, they're very passionate!

Thus Boomers are more issue oriented and committed to focus groups than they are to any particular political party or "umbrella" agenda. Whereas my father voted for Republican candidates until his dying day, I am one of many registered "independents," voting for any candidate that best represents what I believe are the most important issues at the time. Gone are broad, assumed, and generalized political commitments. In their place are targeted but not-to-be-assumed passions. In this regard, J. Walker Smith defines Boomers somewhat cynically as "comfortably righteous."[4] They rally around causes that directly affect them, gather with others who agree with them, and act in accordance with patterns that promote their personal well-being.

It is interesting and of more than small concern that one of the models used in political campaigns for identifying voting groups in this age category is shopping habits. For instance, if you visit the website www.applebeesamerica.com, you can take a quiz that will, with a high degree of probability, predict your political leanings. The underlying criteria are shopping preferences. Here are a few of the questions:

- At a picnic, would you take out of the cooler Sprite, Pepsi, or Dr. Pepper?
- If you won the lottery, would you purchase an Audi or a Saab?
- If we checked your Internet history, would we be more likely to discover that you have visited an auction site like eBay or a dating site like match.com?

Laugh if you will, but much of the political success of Republicans in 2002 and 2004 is attributed to the use of just such surveys.[5] And why would this surprise us? Starbucks built its entire business model, not on the drinks the company designed for customers, but on those the individual consumers created for themselves. This may explain why denominations have struggled over the past decades while new, independent churches thrived. The constituency of national organizations is broad and diverse, while what has become the megachurch, though great in numbers, is local in its constituency and "unaffiliated" nationally; therefore, it can be and usually is more engaged or detached, at will—more narrowly defined.

Thus, organizations that are national in nature will likely continue to struggle in regard to significant growth simply due to their varying regional constituencies. This requires great tolerance—urban to suburban to rural, left to right, white to blue collar, and so on. So maybe tolerance should be the clarion call—the passionate purpose—around which our mainline churches make their appeal to Boomers. In a sermon recently preached at the Old South Church in Boston, the Rev. Ben Guess hit this on the head when he said, "We must be about unity, not uniformity." You can't proclaim a more Boomer-targeted message than that.

7

Spiritual?

Boomers love to describe themselves as "spiritual" but not "religious," a phrase that baffles, eludes, and sometimes frustrates me. When did these characteristics become mutually exclusive, as though anyone who appreciates "traditional" worship on Sunday morning cannot also experience the Divine while anticipating the "green flash" at sunset on the beach? So, to me, this always feels like a dodge for a belief system that either cannot be articulated or is lacking in depth or shape. But, really, it indicates that in their spirituality, as with other aspects of their lives, Boomers want to individualize their relationship with a "higher power," "greater being," or any other name by which they recognize something beyond themselves. As with so many other elements in their lives, Boomers seek to "tailor" their religious beliefs to their own experiences, perceptions, and needs.

A conversation with nonmember Boomers from earlier in my ministry, who wanted their young son baptized, comes to mind:

"Can you do my kid?"

(Ugh.) "What?"

"Can you baptize our son?"

"Okay, what does this mean to you?"

"Well, we were both baptized"

"Do you have any church connection?"

"No . . . but we believe in God. And our family is going to be in town. . . . It seems like a good time to do this. We just see ourselves (and here it comes) as spiritual, not necessarily religious."

"But baptism is as much about being raised in the church as it is an individual act or spiritual blessing."

"Yeah, and we hear you have a great youth program! We just want him to be able to choose what he believes."

"I understand; so why have him baptized? You can't take it back!"

After more conversation, the parents agreed to think about what was discussed, but they never returned. The interesting conclusion to this story is that I find, years later, our youth program to be "loaded" with those infants who are now adolescents. My point? Those parents did exactly what they said; they permitted their child to grow up with the intent of allowing them to "choose" or "not" how to believe. They saw faith as *personal*, not *institutional*. It wasn't that they were necessarily antagonistic toward the church or organized religion, it's just they didn't view participation as obligatory, like their parents might have. In other words, Boomers ARE spiritual, not religious—which means they seek a faith that is relevant, personal, portable, and able to dialogue with other traditions and expressions of belief. Stated differently, they are not so much antireligious, as they are antidoctrinal—and doctrinal is often how they view organized religion.

As in other parts of their lives, Boomers value knowledge gained through personal experience above that derived from secondary sources (such as reading or being taught about something). Like other "capstones" in their lives, the spiritual quest of Boomers begins with self and is extrapolated from there. They are the generation of experimentation, the countercultural product of social upheaval, seekers of enlightenment "out-of-the-orthodox" box, whether through hallucinogenic drugs or New Age perspectives. Most of all, they want to *be*, not *be told* about most everything, including spiritual matters. Once again, Walter Isaacson's interviews with Steve Jobs (a self-styled Buddhist) may summarize this best:

> Religion is at its best when it emphasizes spiritual experiences rather than received dogma. The juice goes out of

Christianity when it becomes too based on faith rather than on living like Jesus or seeing the world as Jesus saw it.[1]

Individualistic—intimate—fluid—emotionally involving and personally satisfying—these are the touchstones of Boomer spirituality. Like Moses speaking with God on Sinai, the fire is real, the heat tangible, the energy empowering, but the flames are ever changing. To understand this is to relate to Boomers where they are at any given point on their personal journey. This is where their discussion begins.

I must add a caveat, however: in spite of what I have pointed out, statistics still reveal that a significant number of Boomers (43 percent) consider themselves "strong" members of their faith tradition.[2] This appears especially true in two specific cases: (1) theologically conservative traditions where there is a strong and constant emphasis upon preserving the "traditional" family, and (2) areas where a strong "identity" has been formed around clear liturgy, clear mission and message, and strong interpersonal connections.[3]

The challenge presented to mainline churches by these observations is not to confront or conform to what, on the surface, appears to be working (such as contemporary worship, strong use of technology, conservative political leanings), but what lies underneath— clear causes, specific responses, a passionate application, intimate relations (such as small focus groups), and a unashamed appeal to the emotional, not just intellectual, aspects of our faith. And when I stop to think about it, wasn't Jesus more focused on people's personal spirits than their temple practices? That is, didn't the needs and issues of individuals take priority over the institutional practices of the temple tradition? Faith was fulfilled in tender touch and compassionate living. To be successful in reaching Boomers, perhaps we should revisit that.

8

FAMILY ORIENTED

As young parents, Boomers wanted their children to experience every opportunity possible. The result was soccer clubs, preschools, space camps, and multiple municipal recreation centers. As mentioned many times previously, a major thread tying Boomers together is their commitment to family. They are often the first in line for any effort (youth mission trips, assistance programs, and the like) related to supporting children or youth. Their own children may have grown up and left home now that they approach retirement, but this sense of commitment and responsibility toward youth and children has not diminished.

This passion, however, presents a two-edged sword, as one of the greatest stresses expressed by Boomers in multiple surveys is their strong desire to assist their children as they go to college and/or graduate and struggle to find a job in a weak economy. Given the downward economic trend of the last several years, many have witnessed their own net wealth decline while watching the cost of a college education rise.[1] Managing this commitment to their children—and now grandchildren—may be the biggest hurdle Boomers face as they move toward retirement. This stress is augmented by the fact that they will probably be living longer, sandwiching them between the support of their children and aging parents.

> Thanks to advances in life expectancy, 71% of today's boomers have at least one living parent and two thirds

(68%) are aiding an adult child financially, either as the primary (33%) or secondary (35%) source of support.[2]

I found this most challenging in my life as circumstances required me to care for a parent declining from Alzheimer's while working to support my children as they completed high school, then college. It was physically, emotionally, and spiritually draining! Topping it off were the haunting questions "Whose going to take care of me when I grow old? Where will those resources come from?" And given the high divorce rates, declining family sizes, and movement of children farther away from their parents for reasons of employment, these are questions that will continue to plague many Boomers.[3]

This means that just as this generation sought congregations that provided family support in their years of parenting, so they will seek assistance in their latter years as they care for their parents and eventually need more care for themselves. How we empathize, anticipate, and address this Boomer need will be critical for our churches in the future. It will certainly play an increasing role in determining our relevancy—maybe even our fate.

9

EVENT-RELATED GIVERS

During the 1990s, when the economy appeared robust (along with American spending), it was far easier to ask Boomers for money than for time. Time was the most precious commodity in their possession, and it was spent going, doing, being, especially when it came to their families. Hence, the birth of minivans, the prevalence of "soccer moms," the growth of first-class preschools and wide variety of after-school programs. Unlike previous generations, who in my experience thrived on attending the general activities of the church (such as potlucks), Boomers were far less motivated to continue these patterns. However, plan an event that was cause specific, personal in nature, community related, and clearly articulated, especially if related to children—doubly so, if said children were their own—and they would generously commit time, energy, and financial resources. I personally witnessed this, time and time again.

This shouldn't surprise us; after all, these responses correlate directly to many of the characteristics we have previously identified. Nonetheless, most of our church financial efforts are still built upon the past model of encouraging our members to support the church because . . . of course, *it is the church!* Which isn't an argument that resonates with or motivates most Boomers. Remember, this generation's most formative years were in the shadow of Vietnam and the wake of Watergate; it is intrinsic to their nature to question and inherent to their spirit to be suspicious of institutions and those who lead them. So why would we expect them to *just give?* Or at least give to their fullest capability?

A study by MetLife done by Boston College's Center for Retirement Research anticipates an intergenerational transfer of wealth totaling $11.6 trillion, including some $2.4 trillion that has already been gifted.[1] Where this transfer of wealth has already occurred, charitable foundations have often been established, from which Boomers are willing to support endeavors they consider worthy, but with very specific criteria.[2] To reach these individuals, as well as encourage overall giving, church leaders must become far more proactive, building relationships, clearly defining causes and ministries, and increasing the involvement of members in the planning and implementation of the ministries they are asked to support. "It's wrong to look at this as a money problem," according to Mark Ottoni-Wilhelm, a professor of economics at Indiana University/Purdue University–Indianapolis, who recently led a study on this subject. "The dip in giving follows the involvement pattern. Because people aren't as involved, the giving pattern traces it."[3] Supporting this thesis, William G. Enright, former pastor of Second Presbyterian Church in Indianapolis, now executive director of the Lake Institute on Faith and Giving, states, "Studies show a person's attendance at worship is the single best indicator of overall charitable generosity. Those who attend worship regularly (two to three times a month) are three to four times more generous than those who attend less.[4]

Just look at charitable organizations in your community that are successful. They target specific issues and are clear and concise in each goal and intended outcome, be it the creation of a children's park or an effort to save the manatees. They ask for short bursts of time; they include participants in the planning; they unashamedly request contributions; and they encourage participants to invite their friends and neighbors to support their cause.

A clear example of this occurred one Sunday when our congregation received an offering in support of an annual, well-advertised, Christmas mission effort. During the time for special sharing, a young woman who worked for the child protection agency in our county briefly explained some personal settings and asked for assistance, if anyone was so moved. Now, the congregation had already completed a five-week-long drive to help children during the Christmas season. However, without any of the "prep" work associated with that campaign, this young woman immediately received an amount greater than the annual appeal. Personal—direct—specific! Just another reminder that giving *is never just giving* for Boomers.

The way many Boomers will approach charitable causes in the future will change, given the recent shift in the world's economy. Their net worth has declined in some cases, which will result in less disposable income and working later into life. This may limit their gifts of both time and money.[5] Still, there is a substantial amount of wealth within this generation, and, regardless of economic conditions, Boomer's motivations for giving will remain the same. In response, our challenge is to be specific and clear in our message, intentionally engaging in our planning and implementation, and innovative in our efforts. It is as simple, and as hard, as that!

10

Growing with Technology

Because I am an "early adopter" of most technological innovations, I assumed that my peers would be also. What I have learned, however, is that there is a distinction between "early" Boomers born between 1946 and 1955 and "later" Boomers born between 1956 and 1964 in this regard. Early Boomers use it because *it's there, they can, and,increasingly, they must,* but later Boomers use it because *it enhances, it empowers, and it is,* well, *very cool!* My birthdate (1956) places me on the cusp between these two groups, so I see and feel both sides of this coin. This also makes perfect sense since the two names most prominent and clearly identifiable with this generational divide, Steve Jobs and Bill Gates, were born about the same time. What provides a shared interest, or bridge, between this divide is technology's influence on communication. E-mail dramatically impacted the work and personal life of older Boomers, and with the advent of texting, tweeting, and social networks like Facebook and LinkedIn, this has expanded at an exponential rate, especially as it has become an everyday norm for younger generations. Naturally, if family is important to Boomers, then the tools of communication used by their children or grandchildren becomes increasingly important. So Boomers do what they have always done—adopt and adapt as necessary.

Social network sites use by Younger Boomers (ages 46–55) increased 30 percentage points over the past two years, from 20% in December 2008 to 50% in May 2010, and Older

Boomers (ages 56–64) jumped 34 percentage points, from 9% in 2008 to 43% in 2010.[1]

Now, this does not mean that to be effective congregations should plunge into use of technology. But because of this generational divide, it is important to be in tune with these distinct differences. Technology is seen, especially by older Boomers, as a means of adding to life, not overwhelming or distracting from it. Hence, it is critical that it is used as fully and effectively as possible in regard to disseminating information, but thoughtfully in regard to worship. Let me see if I can clarify these distinctions.

My wife and I recently worshiped in several area churches. Each was from a similar tradition and all were using technology as a part of their service. In some respects we were very moved by the ways technology added to the liturgy, but at times we found ourselves distracted and detoured. For example, the posting of preservice announcements was useful, and the projection of songs made singing easy. But we found the flashing of scripture during the sermon to be a distraction from the "hearing" of the Word, lessening our spiritual connection with the preacher. Images used at various times during the service added to the atmosphere, much like a specifically decorated chancel can. But sometimes they were too "cute" or overpowering. So, what was our conclusion coming away? Less is more. Going to church for worship should be its own "experience" rather than a replication of browsing on the Internet.

In evaluating the use of technology, churches should bear in mind that Boomers were late comers to this medium. They grew up with TV but adapted to other, more personal forms of technology. As doctors or sales reps they learned to carry not one, but two pagers, a cell phone, and eventually a laptop in order to accomplish their work. No wonder they danced like it was the Jubilee year when the Smartphone brought them all together! They appreciate the freedom, flexibility, and connectivity technology provides, but also chafe at its intrusiveness. Boomers are "backpackers," "kayakers," and other private, get-away adventurers. They may love to watch sports on their new LED TV, but they can turn it off, climb on their pricey road bike, and ride away at any time. If they take technology with them, it is to provide directions via GPS or count calories, not to text—in other words, to *enhance that experience, not intrude upon it!* Unlike younger generations who have grown up with this technology and have a hard time living without it (just try to stop a teenager from "texting" under the dinner table), for Boomers it's all about supporting your personal lifestyle. It is meant to enhance, not interfere.

Like the printing press, the invention and advancement of technology is a gift to our age that cannot be ignored. But it is not our messiah, so we must thoughtfully unearth how to use it appropriately in our churches. Generational differences, even within generations, are significant. As we think about our ministry to and with Boomers, it is crucial that we remember this.

11

Cautiously Optimistic

A survey recently conducted by Pew Research indicated that 80 percent of Boomers were dissatisfied with the way things were going in the country. In fact, the survey labeled this Boomer characteristic as "glum."[1] This was not reflected, however, in the majority of my conversations with Boomers. Rather, despite an expressed degree of uncertainty regarding what might lie ahead, there was a calmness in our discussion. "We'll figure it out" was expressed much more often than, "Oh my gosh, what am I going to do?" Where my conversations mirrored the results of the Pew Survey was that my participants agreed that their standard of living would likely be diminished from that of their parents. If they had a serious concern, or maybe a pause for sadness, it was that their children's lifestyle would probably decline even more than their own. Thus I noted a shared awareness of "less" in the future, but no "panic" in regard to confronting it. And even where there was an admission that they might have to work into the later years of their lives, there was disappointment but not great concern. After all, they wanted to stay active anyway. The only variable in this equation was their health. Would they remain physically able to do whatever work was necessary, or chosen, in the years ahead?[2]

What does this mean for ministry? For me it reveals that, though life has not turned out exactly as many Boomers might have imagined, there is still that belief that "we can make it," "we will figure this thing out," and "it will all work!" Adapt—adopt—achieve! Needed for Boomers to accomplish this are not just the tangible tools of program or personal guidance, but the spiritual ones of hope and promise as well. And haven't these always been the centerpieces of our faith? The question is whether the church itself will succumb to the clouds of uncertainty created by declining memberships, a struggling economy, and a challenging cultural environment. Or will we be the bearers of hope for this stage of transition, in our common life, as well as that of this generation?

Hope and promise are powerfully infectious. They don't require large budgets, the latest in technology, or even the most creative programming. They simply need leaders whose core value is that of making "a joyful noise unto God" (Psa. 100:1 RSV). Every congregation, regardless of membership size or operational budget, can do that!

One of my favorite stories surrounds a king whose country is being torn apart by war and civil unrest. Night and day he is tormented by the whirlwind of events swirling around him. He can find no rest or peace. So he summons into his court the most renowned artist of his land, requiring of the artist a painting that could be hung in the king's private chambers so that at least twice a day, in the morning when he got up and in the evening when he retired, he might gaze upon an image that spoke of hope and thereby find the strength to go on.

Several weeks passed, and the artist finally returned. The royal court held its breath as the canvas was pulled away and the anticipated painting revealed. There before everyone's eyes was the most beautiful picture imaginable. It was a pastoral scene with brilliantly lit, blue skies; plush and green rolling hills; and in the center, a cool and gently flowing spring stream. The king at first leaned forward and then, suddenly, jumped from his throne and shouted, "That's not it! That's not what I commanded you to paint! Go, and don't come back until you can bring a drawing that speaks to me of hope. Otherwise, it's off with your head!"

This time months passed before the artist returned, and this time he entered the king's court, not with bold and confident steps, but with those of uncertainty and fear. A hush swept through the castle as the moment came for the painting to be unveiled. This time, the setting was not gentle and calm, but rough and disturbing. The clouds were threatening and the sky dark and dreary as if in the middle or perhaps near the end of a tremendous storm. The landscape was of a canyon comprised of sharp cliffs. And at the bottom of this jagged ravine ran a swift river strewn with rocks and rapids. But within one corner of the clouds there appeared a break, and through that break, ever so faintly, shone a stream of light—a light that descended from the heavens in a ray that did not end until it reached the top of a lone tree poised on the edge of the ravine. And in that tree sat a bird subtly illuminated by the rays of that light, its beak open in song.

Those in the court sat in silence for what seemed like eternity as they waited to see what the king would do. Then he rose out of his throne with an air of peace those about him had not seen for years, and he said, "That's it! That's hope! The ability to sing in the midst of a storm."

We do not choose the times in which we live, just the faith by which we live in them. Hasn't the church always been at its best during difficult times? After all, we are about "good news," aren't we? Then we must confidently offer it again, making this the cornerstone of any program or ministry we might employ. It is the core value that makes all the others work. It is what Boomers want. It is what they need! And it is ours to offer in bright, bold, and refreshing ways.

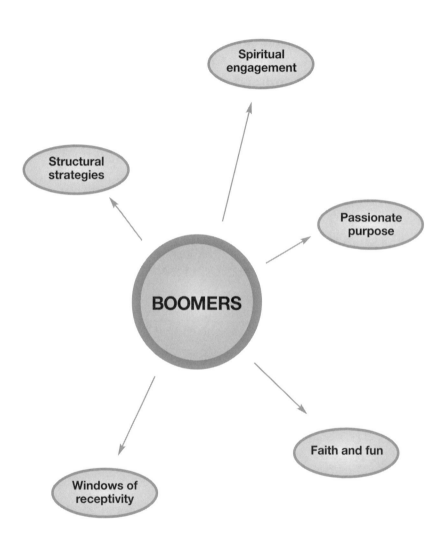

PART TWO

Five Ways to Reach Baby Boomers

In their book *The Stuff Americans Are Made Of,* Josh Hammond and James Morrison share an interesting story about the Danish company Lego and a marketing dilemma it faced a few years back. Although Lego building block toys were popular in the United States, sales were not anywhere near expectations. So the company evaluated, not its product, but the market culture it was attempting to reach. What Lego discovered, comparing sales in Germany against those in the United States, was quite enlightening.

It's a fact that the average American child buys fewer Lego building sets than his German counterpart. Why do you suppose this is? Here is what we know: An American kid tears open a Lego box, tosses out the instructions, and proceeds immediately to create something from his (or her) own imagination. The result has no resemblance to the elaborate and exacting drawings on the box or instruction booklet, it has leftover parts, and it attracts quick praise from the nearest adult. . . . A German child opens the box carefully, finds the instruction booklet, reads it, and takes great care to follow the instructions: blue piece here, red pieces there, yellow in this pile. Then, methodically, with exacting reference to the drawings, he or she builds the first object.

Now here's Lego's marketing problem in America: the American kid takes his initial creation apart, invents something else to his liking, and continues his process until he gets bored and moves on to something else. There is little or no concern for doing it "right." The same Lego kit remains a constant source of invention and creativity. In short, there is little need for another box of Legos.

The German kid also takes his initial creation apart, but there the similarities end. Once the piece is disassembled, he moves systematically through the instruction book to the next challenge. This process continues until all of the possibilities pictured in their instruction booklet are completed. He is now ready for his next kit.[1]

How is this significant? Well, so long as Lego remained insensitive or naive to the culture in which it sought to market, its success was limited. It wasn't until Lego took the time to listen and thus discern the needs of its potential consumers that it discovered innovative methods for meeting those needs.

Applying this insight to the church doesn't mean that we become chameleons seeking to mold worship, preaching, and so on to society as though we were marketing a commercial product. But it does mean that we are challenged to be culturally sensitive in order that the "old, old story" can be offered through contemporary means and ways with integrity. Perhaps this is what the Apostle Paul had in mind, at least in part, when he wrote to the church in Rome saying: "Be not conformed to this world but be transformed by the renewing of your mind . . ." (Rom. 12:2).

Such renewal involves leading by intuition as much as by fact, trusting our leadership abilities at their deepest "gut level" to interpret what we sense is transpiring about us, being willing to take risks in order to confirm what we believe to be true.

I recall a story told at a Convocation for Clergy of Larger Churches in the United Church of Christ a few years back in which a church, due to unfortunate circumstances, was forced to vacate its facility, at least temporarily. It was decided that, rather than rushing back to the old property and its related forms of worship and programming, church members see this time as a "gift" in which to explore alternative ways to worship and provide services not constrained by specific space. In other words, would a storefront or gymnasium not only suffice for worship, but also free resources for other ministries? It was relayed that, obviously, this experiment had its share of "ups and downs."

It was during one of those "down" times that the experiment was called into question at a church council meeting, one member expressing particularly strong concern. The council president, who happened to be an engineer working for NASA's research lab in Cleveland, offered a very powerful response. He said that at NASA Research and Development, there is a 90 percent failure rate, and that the willingness to risk failure is essential to success. If you are not failing at something, you're probably not trying anything new or significant.

Have you ever watched children with a new computer game? They don't read the directions until they've either reached a total dead-end or, more often than not, they've beaten a certain level of the game and are seeking "codes" that provide future short-cuts. How do they accomplish this while most adults are still trying to read page one? They do so by testing their intuition against the data presented on the screen. They push buttons, open doorways, and move up and down corridors until they find the means by which to reach the next level. There is no such thing as failure to them, unless of course, you quit trying. They move forward through active learning, not accepted theory. They believe, as did Edison, that a failed experiment is really not a defeat, but rather the discovery of one more method that didn't work!

In the previous chapters, we have examined, at least in part, characteristics of the Baby Boomer generation, some of which probably resonate with you and others of which you may respond, "Really?" But beneath it all, I believe we share a common understanding that things have changed, and we need to change the way our churches operate. The challenge lies in figuring out what this means—what will work and what won't. Without a doubt, it involves risk. But, really, if our current ministries are not functioning as we hope, then there is far more to gain than to lose.

In the pages ahead, what I have sought to share are some ideas and programs that I have seen work. Of course, they may need to be modified for your particular setting, or they may not be applicable at all. But what I encourage you to do is think about *how they might work.* I have broken them into five areas for ministry that speak to some of the needs and characteristics of Boomers: Structural Strategies (administrative); Spiritual Engagement (worship and individual growth); Passionate Purpose (mission); Faith and Fun (fellowship); and Windows of Receptivity (personal needs). Look them over; share them with your church leaders; and then make a commitment to give something a try. It is, after all, the only way to succeed.

12

STRUCTURAL STRATEGIES

Churches are odd critters, that is, they are caught between two diametrically opposed expectations. On the one hand, people expect them to be the keepers of tradition, but on the other, criticize them if they are not relevant or contemporary. This perception is most clearly expressed by those who come to church several times a year, expecting things to look and feel familiar, like every Christmas or Easter prior, but then throughout the rest of the year complain that the church is stodgy, out-of-touch, and irrelevant.

If one were starting a new congregation, this would be less of an issue because one could build worship, facility, and operational strategies around current needs and ideas. In many ways, this explains the exponential growth of megachurches. Starting from scratch, autonomous, answering to no denominational ties, located in new settings/developments, these churches have minimal or no requirement for continuity with any historic context or external connection. This is completely opposite the make-up of most mainline churches, where a hundred-year history is something to celebrate, but not without baggage of all sorts to constantly work through. A friend laid his finger on this challenge when he said, "People come to church claiming they want to be moved, but are resistant to anything that might move them, literally!" Always sitting in the same place and grumbling when you try a new song or hymn. And then they appear stunned when ecclesiastical rigor mortis sets in.

At least in part, the success of the Willow Creek Community Church, located in Barrington, Illinois, can be traced to its "ground zero" reality. The church started in a downtown movie theatre, then experienced growth into the tens of thousands by focusing on those who had little to no previous church background ("seekers") and those who felt separated from, or hurt by, former religious connections (such as many Catholics). It also didn't hurt that their start was timed perfectly with an incredible growth within that region following Sears' move from Chicago to the Barrington area. But what caught my attention the first time I visited the Willow Creek campus (a complex that looked nothing like my own church facility) was the noticeable absence of any religious symbols, especially the cross. This greatly puzzled me until I heard Bill Hybels say that "symbols, especially the cross, got in the way" of people believing. How? They represented for many too much "baggage from the past." Try to implement that strategy for church growth in our congregations and see how well it works. My point? It is easier to be in tune with the current times when they are your history. It is far more challenging to accomplish relevancy when you represent, and feel accountable to, a century's long, ecclesiastic tradition.

What has been interesting to observe, however, is that even these new churches are not exempt from this past/present–contemporary/historic tension. And this became obvious several years ago when, after the relatively short existence of thirty to forty years, Willow Creek was faced with the challenge of transformation in order to remain vital and relevant. They too were becoming tied to the past, as they had created their own tradition. But, to their credit, they underwent a broad self-evaluation in order to restructure their ministry. No small endeavor given their size. But they did it. A large number of mainline churches need to do the same!

Reaching Boomers is not about mimicking what other churches, those we usually associate with their large numbers, have done. It is not as simple as adding an alternative worship service at a new time. Nor is it as clear as adding a soulful, singing, sandal-wearing guitarist (though this might indeed be one of the outcomes) at the point of the offertory. Rather, it is an intentional examination of what your church is seeking to accomplish by honestly identifying whom you are trying to reach. And in this regard, most churches lack any kind of plan. In our times, ministry needs to be broad in nature, but not generic. We cannot be "all things to all people." Nor should we be! The question is, "Are we doing what is necessary to reach the people we need to reach?" Or are we assuming it will just happen? You can't keep doing the same thing and expect different results. It is important that we honor our traditions, but critical that we rethink how this is done.

Businesses that succeed are those that seek to match their product with specific individuals' needs. This begins, not by throwing some quickly designed "something" on the store shelf, but by understanding the characteristic needs of the market the business is aiming to reach and then creating a system by which meeting those needs is accomplished. Long before Lee Iacocca introduced the minivan or Steve Jobs showcased the iPad, there was the identification of a need and a system designed to meet it. If, indeed, our churches are desirous of reaching Baby Boomers, then we must think in the same way.

We have named many of the attributes of this generation and outlined some of their likes and dislikes. Now, how do we match our ministries with these needs? I would submit that it begins, not with the product, but with the processes or systems behind the scenes that inhibit or enhance what we seek to achieve. For most of our churches, this is no easy or quick fix, but it is a necessary one. So what changes in structure might be examined if we are to evolve into Boomer-friendly congregations?

CREATE BOOMER-SPECIFIC PROGAMS

If possible, hire a staff person or recruit a member to assist in creating/overseeing programming for retired/retiring church and community members. Churches would move mountains to find a youth director. Given the demographic transition of the next twenty years, wouldn't it be prudent to give the same consideration to focusing on reaching Boomers? If a paid staff member is not feasible, discern ways to recruit and develop lay leaders who can fulfill this particular calling.

Form a focus group to oversee ministry to those who are retired and moving toward retirement. This group can help evaluate the success of current ministries in regard to meeting some or all of the identified Boomer characteristics. They could then assist in designing specific efforts, or at least be sure that existing programs contain appropriate elements for attracting Boomers and meeting their needs (for example, a survey of the congregation might reveal a specific or timely desire, such as education about personal finance, health-care matters, or life transitions).

RETHINK AND RENEW OPERATIONS

Rethink how your church operates; update your bylaws and constitution. I am convinced that one reason so many churches struggle is that their basic "rules of engagement" still stem from a perspective of life and society long past. Intellectually, we recognize that lifestyles have changed and families have been dramatically redefined, but the practical ways many churches respond to these alterations lag far behind. Why do we continue to believe that we can effectively operate in the same manner?

Following are some important considerations as you undertake your church's operational "housecleaning":

- Don't plan for the upcoming year based upon what has been done over the past years (for example, a committee shouldn't just do what it feels it must, or what has always been done). Instead, examine what people respond to. Allow participants to review the job description associated with their area of ministry, shaping it into tasks that excite and inspire.

- Avoid simply "filling" constitutionally required positions. Use tools that help match individuals with their passions/spiritual gifts. The job of recruitment may be the single most important task of any church.

- Assign well-defined, short-term tasks and member responsibilities with goals that are clear, concise, and measurable.

Write a covenant that describes what the ministry intends to *be,* and then *do* it.

- Avoid committee terms of two to four years. These no longer fit the mobility and flexibility of a generation that has learned to function "on the move"

- Don't allow people to sit in meetings for hours. Start on time; end on time. If you must have formal meetings, keep them minimal, specific, moving, and outcome oriented.

- Find ways to lessen time spent talking and increase time spent doing.

- Build fellowship time into your agenda. Allow for ways in which people can develop relationships. Just because a committee is task oriented does not mean it is not an important small group. Boomers were all about "teams" in their corporate lives. If necessary, spend time teaching participants how to effectively communicate with one another and the congregation through an appropriate use of electronic tools (such as e-mail and texting). With this in mind, allow them to determine when and how often they will meet. If goals and responsibilities are well established, quarterly gatherings may be all that are required.

- Empower individuals/groups by streamlining their decision-making process. Are members given the freedom to create and implement their ideas, or are they continually slowed by a system that requires approval after approval by a governing body that may not share their excitement? Every minister knows that the quickest way to kill an idea is to "committee it to death" or financially "starve" it. In a world that changes as rapidly as ours, the ability to act quickly is imperative for success.

The church has never operated in a vacuum, and when, historically, it thought it did, it struggled. Boomers' experience in the corporate world has taught them to move quickly, perform in small teams with specific tasks, measure results quarterly, and work electronically. Remember Starbucks? That company's success is not based upon providing the perfect drink for each loyal customer, but rather providing the material and tools necessary for each customer to create his or her own "perfect drink," in response to which customers become loyal. In order to effectively involve this Boomer generation, each church must provide the materials and setting for members to function in a similar way.

When our church took a hard look at itself, we observed a lot of program overlap and redundancy, meetings that squandered time, and little enthusiasm for repeating the annual . . . whatever-it-was event. The areas that *were* working were those not tied to preconceived functions or expectations. So here's a novel idea—instead of expecting people to fit a model for ministry we struggle to make work, why not empower them to create one that does—one of their own?

PUBLICITY, ADVERTISING, AND OUTREACH

Increasingly, we have found the most effective ways of advertising to be less traditional. Such past tools as newsletters or the "Yellow Pages" are not only less productive, but far more expensive. Instead, we use weekly, seasonal, or event-related electronic "blasts." Knowing that everyone does not use the Internet, we also print a limited number of these "blasts" and distribute them throughout church property.

We have found that seasonal signs and the use of electronic "billboards" can also be effective. Located in high traffic spots, they are eye catching and a bit surprising for the viewer. Two examples, which contain very intentional and generational themes, can be seen in the "Resources" section at the end of this book (page 118). The goal is simply to drive viewers to our website.

During the time we employed electronic billboards, we also asked members to place yard signs with the same logo and message in their neighborhoods. Our website hits increased during these campaigns, as did the number of visitors at worship. Probably the strongest affirmation of this effort is that we now see other churches in our city doing this. A picture truly is worth a thousand words.

You may be able to create your own images/ad campaign. If not, consider using resources provided by a professional marketing agency such as www.outreach.com.

BRIEF, CONCISE TAGLINES

Years ago I was told that if you can't describe your church or share an image of your church's ministry in one sentence, then you probably haven't formulated an identity that can be clearly communicated with your members and broader community. Businesses employ this practice constantly as they market themselves and their products. Federal Express: "When There's No Tomorrow." Visa: "It's Everywhere You Want to Be." Adidas: "Impossible Is Nothing." And who could forget Nike: "Just Do It"? These taglines project an image and provide an invitation to those seeking a specific product. They are a very simple, but important, marketing tool.

Our congregation applied the tagline "A Local Church with a Global Vision" for a number of years. This phrase was intended to express our congregational identity in a concise manner and was posted on our website, worship bulletins, t-shirts, and every other form of publicity associated with our church. It melded members, intrigued visitors, and resonated with Boomers.

Acknowledging an evolution in our church's focus, we have recently begun to consider a new tagline:

... Think Differently.
   ... Serve Passionately.
      ... Act Faithfully.
         ... Live Joyfully!
           —Pass-a-Grille Beach Community Church

Both phrases paint a public picture of our church. Both phrases have Baby Boomers in mind.

In my personal search, I was amazed at how many churches did not employ this simple marketing tool, and I suspect that where it was used a specific generational audience was not necessarily given consideration. In others words, yes, they express who the con-

gregation is, but . . . to whom? Nonetheless, I found several examples I liked and thought might have an appeal for Boomers:

- We Agree to Differ. We Resolve to Love. We Unite to Serve.
  (Plymouth United Church of Christ in Des Moines, Iowa)
- Compassion into Action. (Mount Bethel United Methodist
  Church, Marietta, Georgia)
- Informed by the Past. Involved in the Present. In touch with
  the Future. (Faith United Church of Christ, Windsor, Col-
  orado)

A seven-step process for developing a tagline for your congregation can be found at http://www.willmancini.com/2011/02/how-to
-develop-a-compelling-gospel-centered-tagline-for-your-church
.html.

SPIRITUAL GIFTS INVENTORY

Church leaders recognize that an active volunteer base is needed
for their congregation to function, but they fall short in accomplishing this in the most productive manner—productive not just for
the church, but for the spiritual growth of individuals. Performed
in what is often a very subjective manner, nominating committees
coerce friends, guess at new member talents, and randomly recruit
individuals based on arbitrary or selective encounters. The result?
People are invited to join ministries that neither match their gifts
nor feed their souls. Operating within the constraints of an all-too-
dated constitution, nominating committees find themselves filling
job/committee descriptions that are possibly no longer needed,
uninspiring, and seemingly irrelevant—all of which run contrary
to what attracts and motivates Boomers.

This is less the case in "evangelical" traditions where the goal
of identifying spiritual gifts, distinct from personality traits,[1] is
taken very seriously. Although gifts and personality traits are not
necessarily mutually exclusive, there is a key difference—personality traits tend to be about how *you* act or why *you* do what you

do, while spiritual gifts are about discerning the strengths *God* has provided, in order to do what *God* has called you to do. Simply put, the difference comes in the emphasis and order of the words *God* and *you*. Ephesians 4:11–12 strikes at the heart of this subject, listing not just "gifts of the spirit" but the challenge for church leaders to empower people to use them. With this distinction between spiritual gifts and personality traits in mind, Max Lucado writes, "Can you be anything you want to be? I don't think so. But can you be everything God wants you to be? I do think so. And you do become that by discovering your uniqueness."[2]

In *The Purpose Driven Life,* Rick Warren outlines what he interprets to be these "gifts" in five categories he labels S.H.A.P.E.:

Spiritual gifts—the unique abilities that God has given for us to share love and serve others

Heart—the specific passions God has placed in you to glorify God

Abilities—the set of talents God gave you at birth for a specific use/purpose

Personality—the special way God wired you to navigate life, fulfilling your purpose

Experiences—Those positive and painful parts of your life that God would use in great ways[3]

In a supplemental text, written to further explore these five categories, Erik Rees divides them into twenty more specific areas.[4] The twist involved in this approach is its focus on the individual's growth rather than the institution's need. Based on all we have examined, we must surely see that a focus on spiritual gifts would not only be of benefit to our churches as they seek to meaningfully involve volunteers, but would be especially attractive to Boomers, who may or may not be about the institutional church but most assuredly are about their personal growth and its application.

This became clear for me during a discussion with Jerry Angelo, the former general manager of the Chicago Bears. Recently separated from that job, Jerry found himself asking, "What next?" At an age where "retirement" was a distinct option, Jerry was at a point where he could say "Enough!" and settle into the sunrise and sunset walks of "beach life" in Pass-a-Grille. He had earned it! But he was neither physically nor emotionally ready for that. There was a desire, at this "in-between" point of life, to do something. To do more. He had passions. He certainly had past knowledge, experiences, and connections. But what to do? And more importantly, what might God be calling him to do? This is where a program directed at identifying spiritual gifts would help. Would it lead him toward greater involvement in the church? Maybe. The point, however, would rather be to provide a tool for him to discover new meaning and purpose in life. God's purpose. What better gift than that?

Anyone interested in developing a program to help people discover their spiritual gifts and match them with some kind of passionate purpose should look carefully at the options. A number of approaches have value but require careful guidance in their interpretation/application. Some are aimed at helping individuals uncover ways to become more active in *ministry through/in the church,* while others open the door for service *outside of the church.*

Both are important, but for Boomers the focus must be that of promoting the individual's spiritual growth, *not* completing the church's nominating lists. The former is personally inspiring. The latter feels suspiciously as if motivated by an institutional agenda. Language and theology can be a barrier to the use of some of these spiritual gifts inventories, but if you are able to overcome these elements, they can become a useful tool for naming an individual's strengths. If nothing more, they are an excellent tool to initiate reflection on one's *purpose* in the final stage of life, especially if used in conjunction with a mentoring relationship or small group.

One resource I found interesting was a values self-assessment test that can be taken for free online (although the full assessment and instructor's guide is available for a fee) at www.viame.org. I would categorize this as a values assessment with interpretive benefit in a group setting. Discussing the results of this test with a number of participants made it apparent that it could be applied to particular areas of ministry. For instance, the top strengths of one individual, including spirituality, creativity, and the love of learning, suited that person well for promoting new programs, aiding in the creation of alternative worship services, or developing educational events/retreats. Discussion also revealed that this same individual would not find sitting on the church council, or any kind of board, very satisfying. More than likely, it would produce the opposite effect. Another participant's results revealed such strengths as kindness, caring, and a love for visiting new places and meeting different people. No wonder this person was passionate about creating international work/mission trips. (*Now, Discover Your Strengths* is another good assessment tool.)[5]

Another approach is that of Kevin and Kay Brennfleck in *Live Your Calling.*[6] This resource could be used individually, but would definitely be of greater value in a group setting, where exploring life and discerning one's calling in a time of transition could be enlightening. It includes multiple self-assessments that aim at developing a life map for retirement. In my conversations, the need for assistance in this area was expressed repeatedly, as Boomers had no real plan for transitioning toward retirement other than managing their finances. Nor had they given much consideration to how their personal skills and desires might dovetail with God's calling.

Whatever resource you use, these spiritual/personal assessment tests can be of great value. Using these tools will not only assist individuals in this transitional period, providing an important ministry in itself, but potentially broaden your congregation's base of involvement. Does your church have a specific program aimed at helping people map their life into retirement? Because we all should.

ONLINE GIVING, REGISTRATION, AND GENERAL FORMS

Many administrative tasks lend themselves well to the tools of technology. Through group blasts, texts, e-mails, Facebook, or a number of specifically designed software programs, any church can distribute forms, invitations, and reminders for church gatherings or group meetings. These are inexpensive ways to quickly disseminate and receive information, allowing people to read and respond at their own convenience.

The Internet can be especially effective during any kind of stewardship effort, allowing for the inclusion of photos, links to specific articles, archived sermons, and so forth. Responses can be categorized (by weekly, monthly, or quarterly giving, for example) and giving achieved electronically. A December study by Dunham and Company, a firm serving nonprofits, showed that 61 percent of all donors now give online. More revealing is that 50 percent of donors over the age of sixty now give online.[7] The survey names three keys to successful electronic giving:

- Assurance regarding the security of the transaction
- A process that involves a few, simple steps
- Constant clarification regarding what the donor is supporting (Our congregation uses the services of Vanco, www.electronic donations.com/, to support electronic giving; another source for innovative technology is www.acstechnologies.com/, formerly owned by Zondervan).

Of course, teaching your congregation how to use these resources is critical to their implementation. I suggest offering sessions after a Sunday worship, providing information on the sanctuary screen prior to worship, printing written steps in the worship bulletin, or all of these methods. Emphasize how critical it is for every participant to adjust the spam protection on their home computer so that it allows church e-mailings to be received rather than dumped into the receiver's trash.

The core to all this (notifications, invitations, solicitations, and the like) is a well-maintained database that records not just giving, but all areas of interest and participation. For example, if those attending a specific event (perhaps highlighting an outside speaker, Bible study, or Habitat for Humanity) provide an electronic address, they can personally be notified the next time a similar activity occurs. The same thing can apply to any donation made to a specific cause. Since Boomers appear more likely to contribute to specific endeavors about which they feel passionate, this provides an effective means to reach them in a direct manner regarding matters close to their hearts.

This can be especially effective when responding to emergencies or natural disasters, where people are moved to respond quickly and their place of residence is less important than their connection with an institution/conduit they trust. In a setting such as Florida, where visitors have a unique, seasonal relationship with a church, this is critical. Regardless of your church's location, any information you can gather from visitors or seasonal worshipers cannot help but provide a broader reach that can create a good partnership throughout the year.

WEBSITE AND SOCIAL NETWORKING

Websites provide the most affordable means of presenting a "public face" to any community. I am continually surprised, however, at how poorly congregations manage and utilize this resource. Information is rarely updated, or worse, completely outdated. Pictures are canned, and beyond their "homepage," churches often provide little that is enticing to the viewer. Yet this is the first place most people go when looking for a church. So what characteristics make for an effective website?

Easy to navigate. The site should not be cluttered or overwhelming, but rather flow intuitively, leading the viewer from initial points of interest deeper into your site. I have visited several websites of churches that obviously provided dynamic programming but unfortunately attempted to cram *everything* onto their homepage. It was not just overwhelming, but distracting. I moved on!

Inviting. Past events provide a feel for the church, but upcoming activities offer an invitation. Pictures are critical, but video is becoming even more so. A professional in this field relayed to me that viewers are fifty times more likely to click on a video than a still photo or text. Interesting! This could be a personal welcome, intro-duction to the church, or worship clip. Keep it short! Video that is lengthy to load is less likely to be viewed. Give it some entertain-ment value. Remember, "You never get a second chance to make a first impression."

Informative. It's not just a matter of what ministries are displayed, but when and where. Describe your style of worship. List your small group ministries. Provide directions and specific meeting lo-cations. Post your mission/vision statement or tagline. Do you have a safety policy for children? Furnish a reason for visitors to return to your website. Supply links to other sites with articles of interest; provide a weekly pastoral blog or book review. I have found people to be intrigued by what I am currently reading—books, articles, re-views. Use these to your church's benefit as you offer an impression of your congregation while initiating a virtual relationship that opens the door for a more personal relationship.

Including a call to action. This is something on your home page that requires the viewer to connect with you, usually by requiring some information. For example, "If you are interested in receiving more information" or "if you would like to view this month's newsletter," or "if you'd like to hear a few words about this Sunday's message," then. . . . These are sometimes referred to as "opt-in" boxes. In a business context, this is where tabs are placed that offer a "free month's subscription" or to "see a sample."

Online publications often employ this strategy by providing a teaser headline or introduction to a story, but to *read more,* the viewer must register an e-mail address. The goal is to engage the viewer while gathering data that allows you to create a connection. Some churches send personal greetings or notice of upcoming calendar events to those who click on their "welcome" button and register (for an example of a business doing this, visit IncyteMarketing.com).

Honest impression of your congregation. Are the pictures and mes-sages highlighted? Are they aimed at a general or specific target audience? Remember, *a website is not simply a website!* Be true to who you really are. Know the audience you are trying to reach. This is why "canned" websites may be inexpensive or cool, but unrealistic. Since my church is located on Pass-a-Grille Beach, we intentionally set our website to portray a soft, relaxed environment that reflects and appeals to our demographics. An urban, hip image might have been catchy, but untrue. A website that I found particularly intriguing was www.brookhills.org. The Church at Brook Hills (in Birmingham, Alabama) clearly knows its identity and provides multiple points to engage the viewer with very effective "calls" to specific involvement in discipleship. Click on their "Disciple-Making" tabs to view how easy they make it to become involved in groups and mission events.

Optimization of your site. In simple terms, this involves the metadata on the backside of your website that enables you to get a top spot in search engine results. The key here is to find a niche for your site. For example, if you would like to reach Boomers, then start creating content on your pages, blogs, and social media centered on words like "volunteer adventures" or "purpose in retirement." An excellent tool for evaluating the effectiveness of your website is Google Analytics. This will keep track of the number of people who visit your website, what pages they viewed, where they came from, and, most importantly, what keywords they used to find you. (It is also of value to be registered not just with Google maps, but Google Places.)

In this regard, it is also important that you offer links from your site to other agencies or missions you support, but also that viewers of those sites are directed to you. For example, if you actively assist Habitat for Humanity or a local food bank, then be sure they list and link to your site. In this way, viewers will discover common connections and interests. The back door to any church, even if a virtual one, is as important as the front door.

I cannot emphasize enough the importance of this "metadata," or what exists (or doesn't!) behind the scene of any website. Unless the backsides of your site pages are tagged with appropriate titles, headings, keywords, and descriptions, Internet browsers may or may not be directed (both intuitively and inadvertently) to your church site. Uncovering what these keywords are may not be as simple as it sounds. In fact, a shortcoming of the quick "template" websites that many churches purchase is the lack of such keywords. The cost of employing a professional agency to assist in this regard is relatively low and well worthwhile if you are serious about increasing your web visibliity. Otherwise, you may have the most attractive website imaginable, but no one is viewing it. That would be too bad. Our church uses Incyte Marketing for this service.

Blogs, Facebook, and Pinterest. Blogs are proven to have a dramatic effect on the number of visits to related websites. While on sabbatical, I wrote a quick, daily blog. During that ten-week period, the number of visitors to our website increased nearly tenfold. This could be attributed to the uniqueness of these particular writings; however, based upon responses from outside our normal database, we reached a much larger audience than usual.

Most denominations, and a growing number of churches, post/distribute daily devotionals. My conversations with Boomers have revealed a positive response to the "Still Speaking" articles posted daily by the United Church of Christ. Another example of this was a Lenten devotional posted at www.d365.org/journeytothe cross. Over the years, I have personally subscribed to daily devotionals provided by www.beliefnet.com and "The Upper Room" which also has attached a prayer request site, or chapel, to their webpage, where any viewer can post a specific prayer need at devotional.upperroom.org).

I believe we are also seeing a shift from an emphasis on websites to one increasingly focused on customized Facebook pages. A relevant statistic provided byFacebook is that the fastest growing demographic using Facebook are women ages fifty-five to sixty-five. Perfect! This growing resource provides an easy way to send and receive e-mails, along with invitations to events. It helps members stay connected while traveling. In many respects, it offers for free what used to be found on expensive websites. You can customize pages so they provide direct links to agencies related to your church, and with the option of liking your page, a marketing process begins. Every friend of your friends potentially becomes a friend of your church. Exponential evangelism! Like Google, Facebook provides analytics that are beneficial for effectively managing your site. A handbook for accomplishing this can be downloaded at blog.hubspot.com/social-media-marketing-kit; note that, in providing this information to you, hubspot requires you to "register"—a clear "call to action." (For additional examples of customized Facebook pages, visit Aveda or Round Butte Seeds).

Recently purchased by Facebook, Pinterest is a social networking site that allows individuals to post pictures, stories, and articles on a bulletin board for others to read. For instance, if someone has a particular hobby, like cooking, that you find fascinating, that person can post recipes and you can then view them. This is one more way for people to find and connect with your church. We are using it as a means of posting books currently being read by our staff. However, there are multiple ways that this medium could be used within any church setting.

QR code. QR is short for "quick response," because these codes can be read quickly by a smartphone. They are used to take a piece of information from a transitory media and put it into your cell phone. Once it is loaded to your cell phone, it can provide information regarding your church or a specific ministry. Accessed through a smartphone, it immediately provides key information (location, worship or program times, mission statement, site for donating, and the like) for the viewer. It can (and should) be placed in or on worship bulletins, newsletters, business cards, flyers, t-shirts, and any other visual identifiers your church uses and will probably become increasingly integrated into advertising in the future (multiple sites, such as http://www.qrstuff.com/, can assist in creating a QR code). A sample QR code can be found in the "Resource" section at the back of this book (page 119).

If you're like me, all of this feels very overwhelming, which is why, if possible, your church should recruit a professional to assist in creating your Internet presence. Volunteers mean well but often do not have the time required to effectively accomplish this. Likewise, they can get caught up in their own agendas, missing the big picture or resisting the target audience you hope to reach.

All of this proved true at our church, but what emerged from our struggles was the idea that we could help design and maintain websites and other online presences at a reasonable cost for other churches, perhaps helping them to eliminate some of the problems we faced. In fact, the website of the Florida Conference of the United Church of Christ is one example of our effort. And guess what age group sought to implement this solution for our church and others? Boomers! Just remember, an online presence is an important means of operating in today's mobile society, and it is growing daily, well worth your church's time and resources.

MEMBERSHIP

The word itself sounds static, so no wonder it has little or no appeal for a generation that will forever (whether true now, or not) see themselves as anti-institution and counter-cultural. Belonging "officially" may have appealed to previous generations, but not so much to Boomers. It is why they register as Independents in the political system and, I suspect, one of the implicit attractions for belonging to a nondenominational church. And though the numbers associated with the megachurches are large, their numbers for "members" are often small, well-defined, and built around high expectations (such as tithing and leadership). In these instances, those desirous of a deeper relationship with the church do not join *membership classes,* but participate in *discipleship groups.* The title itself says it all, as the focus is not a closer walk with the church, but with Jesus.

For a long time, I approached membership from the wrong perspective, holding an almost cavalier attitude that when someone had officially "joined my church," the deal was done! And with older generations, except for meeting the standard expectations regarding basic programming and worship, the task of getting them into the church, was complete—*they attended; they pledged; they had committed*. Why wouldn't I think this way? This was the church model I had witnessed and inherited in my career. But Boomers are looking for something different, something more. They may not join, but they will participate. They may not pledge, but they will passionately give.

Our challenge is to not relativize or minimize what they bring, but to seek various ways in which to maximize what they are willing to offer. Currently, most mainline churches offer one route to church membership. We need to consider various, equally valuable routes or levels of connection/participation—virtual, worship related, financial steward, seeker, active visitor, disciple, and so on. Currently I have more questions than answers in this regard; however, the doors remain open as to a solution. I just know that for Boomers, involvement does not equal membership, and understanding this difference is critical to reaching this generation.

STAFFING

It is important not only that we acknowledge the gifts and talents, as well as individual points of commitment, that Boomers bring to our congregations, but that we also bless, anoint, and utilize them. A case in point is the spiritual growth of my own spouse. A high-risk labor and delivery nurse by training, a number of years ago she began to feel a pull away from that area of expertise to one of youth ministry. Because of my position and our obvious connection, I was reluctant to explore her passions and put them to work.

Stereotypes of "the pastor's wife" were vivid in my mind. But when our church blessed and empowered her, our program boomed! Our youth ministry jumped from fourteen to eighteen middle school and high school youth to fifty to seventy, many of whom were not directly associated with our church. One of our biggest outreach programs involves our national and international youth mission trips each summer. Given that the demographics of our Florida location are skewed toward retirees, this is amazing!

Currently, my wife serves not only our congregation in this area but is also a regional youth minister for the Florida Conference of the United Church of Christ. My point? She possessed no seminary degree or credentials of ordination. According to most ecclesiastical standards, she had no "official call." Rather, she possessed gifts, talents, and one characteristic more important than any other—*passion*—for a specific calling. And I suspect her story is just one of many. Applying the tools previously mentioned to identify the spiritual gifts of those we seek to engage, we can—we must—empower servant leaders in our churches.

At a clergy gathering, I once heard Bill Hybels, founder of the Willow Creek Community Church, say that their church never started a ministry unless a core group of lay people were willing to create and lead it. Compare this with a statement made by Robert Schuller, pastor of the Crystal Cathedral, in one of his books, ironically titled *Your Church Has a Fantastic Future!*

There will be no great forward renewal in the Protestant Church until we recognize that dynamic and aggressive leadership is the key. Leadership definitely does not belong in the hands of part-time thinkers. So the place of leadership logically and naturally rests in the lap of the minister and the salaried staff leaders in the church![8]

Today, Willow Creek is still growing, while the Crystal Cathedral is . . . well, need I say more?!

13

S P I R I T U A L   E N G A G E M E N T

As with all areas of ministry pertaining to Boomers, the key word to bear in mind, whether it involves music, learning, mission, or meditation, is "engagement." At what levels are our efforts seeking to "engage" potential participants? Do our services of worship and groups for prayer nurture, challenge, and pique Boomers' interest? Do we issue a clear "call to action"? Are there personal, intimate settings in which to deeply question and explore the faith? Are we taking seriously the scriptural mandate to love God with heart, mind, body, and soul (Deut. 10:12; Mark 2:30, 33; Luke 10:2)? This is what spiritual engagement is about—*connecting with people at multiple levels.* Inviting them into an *experience* of faith, not just a *discussion.* Involving them in the *continuation* of the biblical story, not simply a *recollection* of it. Leonard Sweet writes:

> The Bible is less a book about how people thought about God than it is a book about the religious experience of individuals and communities. Experience is the engine room of the biblical and spiritual enterprise.[1]

The business world seems to understand this, at least those who are successful. Starbucks doesn't market coffee, but the experience of coffee. Similarly, Apple doesn't sell technology, but the convergence of art, technology, and each user. It's about touching, feeling, engaging what's before you—the experience. And if you've nodded "Yes" to any of this, then the question that follows is, "How do we, the church, accomplish the same thing, with many of the same people?"

TIME, TIME, INTIMATE TIME

A number of years back, the *Boston Globe* published an article bemoaning the fact that young doctors no longer knew how to use stethoscopes. They still wore them, almost as a badge of office, but were not really trained in the fine techniques for using this diagnostic instrument. Instead, this generation of physicians opted for more sophisticated technology that led them to the same conclusions at a much higher cost. But the greatest loss identified by this article was associated with this change in physicians' approach to healing—*doctors were no longer simply listening to a patient's heart!*[2]

Any kind of spiritual engagement involves spending time with Boomers in order to really "listen to their hearts." This means intimate conversations over coffee, at lunch, at beach parties, and so forth—meeting them "where they are." It is in these personal settings that questions can be asked, ideas challenged, perceptions overcome, institutional concerns abated, and relationship(s) created. Too often, our strategy is based upon people coming to us. And over the years, it is my observation that pastors spend less and less time one on one with parishioners. We certainly do not make the home visitations we once did. How contrary to Jesus eating and drinking in the homes of those outside accepted religious norms (Matt. 9:10–11). To reach Boomers, we must go into their world, rather than expecting them to come into ours.

My son is a police officer, and one day I decided to have a serious father-son talk, the goal of which was to encourage him to "stay balanced." Seeing all that he constantly did, I was afraid it might jade him regarding human nature. So I said, "Remember, where you work is not the real world." To which he instantly replied, "No, Dad, where *you* work is not the real world!" It may be an extreme example, but it sure opened my eyes. We cannot understand the people outside the church and the world that is theirs by camping, perhaps hiding, in our churches. Jesus said, "Go . . ." and that's where it begins.

SMALL GROUPS

When we look at the ever-growing phenomenon of the megachurch, what one usually notes are the large worship numbers. But if one looks deeper, one usually uncovers a number of small groups settings where participants feed and nurture their personal faith through intimate relations. Growing up in a world that was constantly gravitating toward the "big box" experience, Boomers were drawn toward churches with big worship experiences and the broad variety of programs that large numbers can provide. But the deeper connections and lasting commitments are almost always tied to a more personal place of engagement.

I first observed this while pastoring in Chicagoland, beneath the broad shadow of the Willow Creek Community Church. My oldest daughter, who was at the time in fourth grade, had a classmate who suddenly succumbed to heart failure and was rushed to intensive care, in need of a transplant. Because of her relationship with my daughter, I made a number of calls on the family even to the day when they placed the girl in a drug-induced coma in a final effort to buy time, in the hopes that a heart donor might be found. Unfortunately, one was not.

During the entire time she was hospitalized, not once did my visits coincide with that of a minister from the Willow Creek Church. This is not to say that a visit from an "official" minister of that church never occurred—I'm sure it did—but rather to emphasize that the main source of that family's spiritual support came from members of their church's "small group." Although worship and programming were important to this family, it was very apparent that this "small group" was their primary point of connection and spiritual engagement.

At Pass-a-Grille Beach Community Church, it is through our small group ministries that our greatest individual growth, spiritual nurture, and eventually church leadership has emerged. Ebbing and flowing, based on the availability of staff and trained volunteers, 10–15 percent of our people have been involved in such a group. Small groups come in many shapes and sizes (prayer groups, Bible or book study groups, and so on), but when I speak of them, I am talking about a specific program that takes people deeper in the faith. We have found the Upper Room Series entitled *Companions in Christ* to be a great asset in this regard. Theologically as well as practically, this series works well in our church, building lasting, intimate relationships for sharing, caring, and the deeper exploration of faith that Boomers seek.

SEAMLESS, INTIMATE, EXPERIENTIAL WORSHIP

What is this? Well, to be honest, we are still in the process of discovering what it means. In some ways, it is like contemporary worship, but not. In other ways, it reflects traditional worship, but not necessarily. What *does* it involve? The best way for me to describe my perception is from a walk I experienced through the temples of ancient Egypt. Whether moving through the depths of Abu Simbel or standing at the center of the great Hall at Karnak, I was drawn into that religio/culture by the pictures, images, and carvings that seemed to surround and embrace me *in their story*. And even though I could not read the hieroglyphics, I felt a part of the setting—included in a narrative that somehow made we feel like it was my own.

This was a stark contrast to my experience at the Vatican. There, I felt overwhelmed by paintings taken from here or there and sculptures done by this or that artist—I truly suffered a severe case of "stimulus overload." Even though images around me in the ancient Egyptian temples were great in number, they seemed to flow with a story, whereas the artwork of Rome felt disjointed. Don't misunderstand me; it was impressive, but in a more segmented, piece-by-piece way. And that's not the experience of worship we were seeking to design.

Our intent was to avoid the frequent "stops" and "starts" that most worship services contained, even our own, so as to create a liturgy that flowed from start to finish. Surrounding the worshiper with sight, sound, and intentional movement, our goal was to lead them seamlessly, and intuitively, from the invitation to worship to the benediction. A good movie captivates its audience with theme and pace from beginning to end. Worship should do the same. The goal is not "Wow, that was a great sermon" or "What an outstanding choir anthem" but rather "You know, I really felt a sense of grace today."

Addressing this goal, Leonard Sweet writes, "Jesus' goal was not that everyone understand him, but that everyone experience him. Jesus creates space in which (people) can enter into divine mystery and dangerous grace."[3] Can someone experience God in our worship without prior knowledge of what to do and when? Can people feel the spirit of Christ without having to explain it? And finally, does our worship have clear focus that provides tangible meaning?

One of the great gifts of Apple's approach to technology, for people like me, is that I can pick up their product, be it a phone, laptop, or tablet, and immediately appreciate it without having to read any directions or know any key combinations. When I taught preaching to seminary students, I told them that the ultimate measure of any sermon was whether it met the listener's question of "So, what?" So what . . . does it matter? So what . . . does it mean? So what . . . do I do now?" We asked ourselves these questions in seeking to design a worship experience that met the needs of a Boomer generation.

So how did this worship format look? What was included? A few highlights are outlined in the following list. A copy of our worship bulletin that contains both our early (nontraditional) service and our later (traditional) service can be found in the "Resources" section at the back of this book (pages 119–20):

- Shorter, tighter service, forty-five minutes in length. Early service begins at 8:45 A.M.; second service follows at 10:00 A.M. People love gathering early so they have more time in the rest of their day.

- Intimate and personal atmosphere. Communion is served at every service, by intinction, with a personal blessing. On the Sunday in Epiphany, when our lectionary passages were about the baptism of Jesus, we substituted a renewal of baptismal vows, using a symbolic touch of water. As worshipers came forward to receive their personal blessing, joyful tears were abundant.

- Use of more contemporary language, especially during communion.

- No "offertory." Rather, when worshipers come forward to receive communion, we have offering receptacles available so they can leave an offering. The flow is designed to link your "offering" (response to God's call) with the gift of grace (bread and wine).

- Keyboard soloist as primary musician. The music is contemporary, or an updated version of an older tune. It has a "bluesy" kind of "rock" beat but is not loud. Music is more meditative in nature. Language can often be a hurdle in the use of contemporary music. There are some very good resources, including *Sing! Prayer and Praise* by The Pilgrim Press. We are also blessed that our instrumentalist is able to write songs that go specifically with the scriptural text for the message. (Just a note: If you're wondering where to find a musician for such a service, go to colleges or other established music programs. But don't overlook your local pub. Not only have we found musicians in such places, but some have eventually joined our church.)

We have not replaced worship bulletins with overhead projection for songs but may do so at some point in the future, primarily because the space required for printing words limits the amount available for "call and response" prayers and other items in the liturgy. We have, however, used the screen to show an image or video that ties to the worship theme. (You can make your own slides or use resources available at providers such as www.sermons.com or www.theworkofthepeople.com.)

We think very carefully about our bulletin graphics, and the inside center of the 11-by-17-inch trifold allows for a personal message for one of our ministers.

Here are a few additional ideas that we have found to be successful in our efforts to create engaging, experiential worship:

- We held a series of worship services based on the "I am" passages from the Gospel of John. On the Sunday when the text read, "I am the bread of life," we lined the sanctuary with bread makers so that the air was filled with the aroma of homemade bread. When the text read, "I am the vine and you are the branches," worshipers were given a cut-out leaf upon entering the sanctuary. At the conclusion of worship they were invited to complete a task during the week that bound them closer to Christ's ministry. They were then asked to write a word or phrase on that leaf that summarized their action, and then return the next Sunday, where their leaves were used to complete a beautiful mural of vine and branches on the sanctuary wall. It was exciting to watch participants as they visually created an offering that celebrated how their individual acts of ministry blended to form an image of "the body of Christ."

- On Epiphany, the Sunday we recalled the baptism of Jesus, a large water fountain was placed on the chancel that bubbled water during the service.

- During Lent we erected a cross, upon which we invited worshipers to place prayers during the Lenten Season, in the same way that visitors to the Western Wall in Jerusalem feel profoundly close to God by leaving written notes (see the photo on page 120 in the "Resources" section). The positive response of our people was overwhelming as, week after week, more and more notes covered that cross.

- On Pentecost, we not only hung red banners and streamers throughout the sanctuary, but also had in place a beautiful patio, altar-like, propane-fed fire that burned through worship. The Acts 2 text was read simultaneously in six languages, creating a cacophony of sound. (See the photo on page 120 in the "Resources" section.)

- One Communion Sunday, worshipers were invited to come forward and break a piece of bread from one of the ten loaves contained "inside" a six-foot cross.

- An exciting Easter worship one year involved individuals being given a carnation. During the time for offering they were invited to come forward and weave their carnation into a large cross made from chicken wire. As the closing hymn was sung ("Christ Is Risen Today"), the cross, attached to cables, was raised before the congregation.

- Weekly, we try to create a chancel that visually adds to the morning's scripture and worship theme. In this regard, we have used everything from diving tanks (theme: "diving deep") to a small rowboat (theme: fishing for disciples).

- A sermon that is recalled time and again is one in which I portrayed the street sweeper who followed Jesus' parade on Palm Sunday. I do not recall where I got this idea, but it had a profound impact on the congregation and can be viewed by going to www.youtube.com/embed/gULJ6MIi9eo. Similarly, my associate and I did a Lenten series entitled "Characters of the Cross," where we, in first person, presented such individuals as Mary, Caiaphas, Pilate, and others.

- Finally, seeking to be true to our identity of being a "learning church," we try to weave into our worship a brief exegetical introduction to the scripture. Understanding the hows, whens, and whys of the early church, or temple practices, or Mt. Sinai itself, helps the worshiper to step into the story. I'm not sure how I feel about the feedback in this regard, but it goes something like this: "Your sermons are wonderful, but what I really love is the exegesis before scripture."

All of these services were fun to plan and lead. Each proved meaningful to those in attendance, allowing them to experience the scriptures, not just hear them. And the "buzz" around the community that soon developed was, "I love coming. You never know what's going to happen." (Visit www.experientialworship.com/ideas .html for more ideas.)

SUNDAY MORNING LIVE: STREAMING WORSHIP

One factor that attracted me to my current congregation was their interest in doing some form of ministry online. This is no longer a "futuristic" idea, but nine years ago, it was cutting edge. Through the generosity of someone's estate, we were able to purchase the equipment that enabled our church to record, edit, distribute, and broadcast our worship. And though this form of ministry can be limited due to each church's finances, anyone can participate by using resources such as YouTube.

Now, some of you are already listing the ways in which this doesn't qualify as worship, but bear in mind, this isn't intended to replace worship, just extend it.

Here is one example of what we have experienced: Mark and Karla, a couple visiting seasonally, began viewing our worship online when they were at their primary home in Memphis. As we encourage viewers to respond to sermons online, there began a dialogue that developed into relationship. When they decided to renew their wedding vows, I was the minister they invited to officiate, even though they were seven hundred miles away and had a local church connection. Later, when the opportunity arose to relocate for work, the relationship they had developed with our congregation became a significant consideration. While I recognize that many things were a part of their final decision, my point is that we were "in the mix" because of the relationship created online. Today, they are active members of our church.

Other examples involve several weddings and a memorial service. At the conclusion of one wedding (streamed live), I was dismayed to find the bride's mother talking on her cell phone in our narthex, crying. My first thought was, "Whose name did I mispronounce?" What she shared, however, was how the bride's grandparents had been unable to attend the ceremony due to poor health, but had watched the service online. "We are so very, very, grateful," she told me.

On another occasion, the groom was originally from South Dakota, and the bride, Venezuela. On the day of the wedding, friends and families from both settings, though thousands of miles apart, we able to come together for that celebration. And how interesting it was to watch our viewers' "chat boxes" light up in Spanish.

The memorial service was much different. A member of the community had died, and the one child who lived locally inquired if we could perform a service. Why? Because she knew we could stream it online. It was their intent to do something for family who were scattered around the world. "Would you help us gather, if only virtually?" Which we did—me, the organist, a daughter and her husband, and the cameras. Online you would never have known these were the only people in attendance. But that didn't matter; the family had connected in a way otherwise impossible. And a note posted on our "chat room" wall says it all, "I'm glad we could worship together, even if only online." Odd, yes, but relevant to our times.

PRAYER VIGILS, LABYRINTH WALKS, DRUM CIRCLES

Our church has a beautiful brick labyrinth that provides a wonderful setting, not just for private walks, but for special or seasonal worship. Because it already has the feel of "sanctuary" space, it is a wonderful tool for services of a more intimate nature. On multiple occasions we combine the labyrinth walk with brief worship or service of Holy Communion. If you do not have access to a permanent labyrinth, portable ones are available at a minimal cost. The labyrinth appeals to Boomers on a number of levels because it is active, but quiet; private, but also communal.

Similarly, our church is located within several hundred feet of the beach, thereby providing the most beautiful of natural sanctuaries. At various times we have worshiped on the shore with an environmental theme. And at other times, we have begun worship on the beach and processed into the sanctuary. Drum circles are also a popular expression of spirituality in our area. Thus, steel drums can provide an appropriate addition for an outdoor gathering. My point is to use the resources available to you. The environment, Earth Day, Arbor Day—all have significance for Boomers. Whether at the beach, in the mountains, in a grain field, or at downtown city park, we should faithfully use the sanctuaries God has provided.

E-READERS, LINKS, AND ONLINE LEARNING

Boomers represent the highest level of education in U.S. history, with 88.4 percent having completed high school and 28.8 percent holding a bachelor's degree or higher.[4] Hence, continued learning is important. The challenge to meeting this need is simple—time. This may explain the growing popularity of eBook readers such as the Kindle or Nook. It fills this need and meets this challenge, simply and effectively. A recent survey by *Affinity Magazine* reports that Boomers (ages fifty to sixty-four) are 19 percent more likely than other age groups to own an eReader, and later Boomers are increasingly gravitating toward tablets like the iPad.[5] But owning one of the devices is secondary to what they represent—reaching a generation that loves to learn and read but is constantly on the move.

So, rather than relying on a pedagogical model where participants meet at a specific time and location, more and more churches are moving toward recorded/cached presentations that can be viewed at each participant's discretion and then discussed in a class-style format in person or online. Webinars fill this need to a degree, but only in part, as they still require being in front of a computer at a designated time. Now, I accept that this format this does not have all the advantages of traditional "face-to-face" learning, but innovations in software applications lend themselves to incredible interaction between presenter and participants. And given the choice between minimal and increased participation in learning opportunities, I would opt for the latter. (Check out www.youversion.com, which has created a mobile "app" for streaming worship or a Bible Study, with notes, on any mobile device for free.)

Our church began exploring this medium in several different ways. One was partnering with seminary professors, who recorded presentations related to the lectionary seasons, which were posted online along with a downloadable study guide. Individuals could watch the presentations at their own convenience, with discussion to follow in either a face-to-face or online setting. Access to equipment or seminary instructors may make this unrealistic for many churches, but pastors can accomplish the same thing by combining their theological knowledge with a laptop and a little work. Personally, I believe this would be a great area for churches, denominations, and related seminaries to partner, increasing their reach in the most cost-effective manner possible. The growth of iTunes University and Apple's interactive textbooks is, I believe, evidence of this increasing trend for learning. Another example of online education is the Center for Progressive Renewal (progressiverenewal.org)

In his Faith Formation 2020 initiative, John Roberto takes the position that focusing on the formation of an individual's faith at specific ages or transitions is critical to the vitality of any church. He provides a number of ideas regarding how to accomplish this, centered around creating a "faith formation network" that links to audio/visual, electronic tools of all kinds. His concept is that we build not just learning centers, but clearinghouses for all kinds of ministry, thus connecting people to mission projects, Faith in Art Tours[6], relevant blogs, and commentaries that touch on life transitions.[7] It is a very thoughtful approach to ministry in a new age.

This does not mean that I would abandon traditional forms of learning. Face-to-face gatherings are still best for creating relationships. However, if you are targeting the involvement of Boomers, then careful attention should be given to the materials selected. We have used several series by Rev. Adam Hamilton, senior minister at the Church of the Resurrection in Leawood, Kansas. His mix of study book with accompanying DVD is what I would call a marriage between learning and adventure. He does more than talk about the final forty-eight hours of Jesus' life; he walks viewers through the traditional locations in Israel. Likewise, we have found "The Greatest Story" series, published by Augsburg Press, to be popular, at least in part due to its beautiful and unique visual use of sand artwork by Joe Castillo.

INTIMATE SPACE, READING LOUNGE

Besides coffee, there is a reason Starbucks thrives. In the creation of comfortable space, they have provided a place where people can read, reflect, and informally congregate. This is a concept that can be adopted and adapted by our churches. For years, churches maintained libraries and/or parlors—space in which to read or gather. In too many cases, this concept has declined or lost its appeal—space has become uninviting and the books on the shelves are outdated. What if:

- We modernized our space (easily accessible, rather than some out-of-the-way, unused room)?
- Made coffee available?
- Invested in current books or publications (in our church, members donate their hardback books to our reading room)?
- Displayed new arrivals; publicized a "recommended reading" list?
- Made wi-fi available that connected through our homepage (when a person registered)?
- Shared links to articles of interests, online programs, and so on as a follow-up to each reader's registration?
- Held gatherings for book discussion—made space online to post personal reviews, book reviews, and posted articles?

Boomers are traditionally readers. This is a wonderfully active but subtle way to reach them.

ADVENTURE LEARNING

This involves everything from hikes in the mountains to weeklong trips in the Boundary Waters. It is simply the combination of a unique trip with an opportunity to study, reflect, and spiritually commune with others. It combines three things that appeals to Boomers: nature, individuality within a smaller group, and adventure. Likewise, I have found that pilgrimages (not tours!) to Israel and other sites of religious/spiritual interest deepen participants' faith and build relationships that draw them closer to our church community.

There are few settings that can match reading the Beatitudes on the hills beside the Sea of Galilee, walking the Via Dolorosa, prayer in the prison under Caiaphas' house, or, for that matter, reading the creation story or one of the Psalms at the foothills of the Rocky Mountains. It was interesting and affirming that when I sought to establish a recent visit to Egypt, participants (Boomers) were interested in seeing the Pyramids of Giza, the Valley of the Kings, and so forth, but what they were *excited* about was the nighttime climb to the top of Mount Sinai where they would witness the sunrise.

ACTIVE SPIRITUALITY

This is a simple area in which to initiate a new program. Incorporate or combine exercise—walking, yoga, tai chi, aerobics—with a time for prayer or meditative discussion/reflection. Use the skills and talents available to you in your church or community to accomplish this. Listen and you will discover specific areas of interest. It can, and will, work!

14

Passionate Purpose

The book of Ecclesiastes begins with the words, "Vanity of vanities . . . all is vanity" (Eccl. 1:2), which makes more sense when translated, "Meaningless, meaningless . . . all is meaningless." At first glance this would seem the least likely biblical passage one might use to reach Boomers, but maybe not. Why? Because, if there's one thing in life that Boomers share, it's their insatiable desire to discover a deeper meaning for their existence, and all of life. Never fully satisfied, always looking for "something more," it is no wonder that for years Boomers have been referred to as "seekers." So this text does have significance for this generation—not that of personal insight or inspiration, but rather of challenge.

The problem has been that what the church has offered them for decades was primarily a secondary experience of faith, that is, "Listen, while someone else tells what it means to be a Christian," or "Sit, while someone who *does ministry* presents a slideshow about what he or she is doing as a Christian on your behalf (then we'll take up an offering—your point of participation). I recognize this is probably an overstatement, but as a young adult, and even as a young minister, this is my recollection of how the *real* work of the church got done! Mission and ministry was something another performed and you supported. And this just doesn't appeal to the majority of Boomers who want to directly help others, in ways and through means not yet formed or even conceived. So how do we tap into the possibilities and passions of this generation for ministry? A few suggestions follow:

HANDS-ON MISSION TRIPS

Two observations seem to be very apparent about Americans in general: (1) they are very generous; (2) their interest fades with time. In other words, we struggle with a cultural attention deficit. Any doubt of this can quickly be overcome by watching the rotation of athletic coaches or corporate executives. "What have you done for me . . . this quarter, or this season?" Boomers seem especially susceptible to this chronic attitude. It is why, whether in the areas of giving or committee structure, short-term commitments appear to work better than long-term commitments. This may be why endeavors that require a compact burst of time and energy, but provide a deep sense of satisfaction, have a strong appeal.

The youth ministry at our church is particularly strong, with sixty to seventy weekly participants. One of the reasons for this program's success is the annual mission trip. Every year our congregation helps the youth go for ten days somewhere in the United States or abroad. They have repaired homes in Alaska as well as constructed churches on the Amazon. And the strongest support for this program comes from parents and grandparents who are . . . Boomers. In fact, some of the quickest and easiest money I have ever helped raise occurred when the Peru trip almost "fell through" due to a sudden and dramatic increase in airline costs.

An interesting side effect of these youth trips has been the increased interest of adults to do the same thing. The edginess of a week on the Amazon especially grabbed the attention of Boomers. They too wanted to experience a faith adventure. Thus, when Hurricane Katrina struck New Orleans, they were eager to respond! And did! Since that time, this has been a key point of engagement for this age group in our church.

As I have stated, however, emergency needs and short bursts of time and vivacity seem to have a much stronger appeal for Boomers than ongoing situations involving poverty. I do not wish to generalize in this regard, but our church experienced a definite numeric decline when, after several years of working in New Orleans, we sought to shift our focus and energy to residents of Appalachia.

What we discovered was that we could not assume this energy to be transferable. This doesn't mean that nondisaster or less urgent projects won't succeed, but that the identified setting and accompanying need *are* critical.

As a result of these and other observations, those involved in planning mission events at our church have begun to look at how we can quickly mobilize for disasters. One solution on the table is the rental of motorhomes, along with the purchase of a trailer, for hauling food, clothing, water, or tools. It will be interesting to see how this is resolved. As the old saying goes, "Where there is a will, there is a way." Add "passion," and you've got success! I offer some recommendations for planning a trip based on our experience.

- Find a very organized volunteer, or pay someone to specifically manage your mission trip (find a location, weed through the details, schedule transportation options). Bringing people together from various churches for these kinds of projects is a ministry that denominational organizations might provide more intentionally. Having someone to encourage, recruit, and support volunteers who would not otherwise be able to participate in such a ministry would be invaluable, especially with small churches that might be more reluctant because of lesser numbers (our church is currently working to establish just such a service).

- Use an established organization, if at all possible, for your site location and set-up. They will provide tools, on-site managers, and work specifics. Pay close attention to the skill level and abilities of volunteers in order to match them with appropriate tasks (it will be more fun for everyone).

- Find the best forms of transportation to the location and on site.

- Arrange responsibilities into small tasks (for example, meals, local activities, equipment). In some instances, this can involve people who are not able to do more physical tasks.

- Make devotions an intentional and meaningful part of each day.

- If possible, plan at least one "out-of-the-box" adventure or fun-related activity during the trip.

COMPUTERS FOR KIDS

This project at our church is a wonderful example of the creativity the Boomer generation offers the church. It began with a simple discussion of the cultural and technological changes occurring in our lives and society. The conversation turned to "What to do with my old computer?" and the dialogue went something like this:

"It still works but is quickly becoming obsolete for my personal and professional needs. I could donate it to a charity, but it may not meet their needs either. I can't just throw it away, that feels, well, . . . sinful. What to do?"

"Well, we know that every child doesn't have access to a computer and many families can't afford one. Could a program be created that transferred an available resource from our hands into those of someone who could benefit?

In that instant, the "Computers for Kids" program was born. In theory, it's really quite simple:

- Receive computers from church families or local businesses who are upgrading.
- Identify children without a home computer who would benefit from a computer in their home (we accomplished this in partnership with the local school district).
- Recruit volunteers to tutor students over a specific period on the computers, which have been loaded with the same software as that used at students' schools.
- (and here's the payoff): Send each student home with his or her own computer after each has completed the teaching/mentoring sessions.

It was a tremendous success! Kids who could benefit from this "leg up" did. Boomers who loved technology could put their passions to work fixing the donated computers, teaching others valuable skills, and recycling what had previously been seen as a disposable asset. And with this, the church moved into a relevant and timely mission. As things stand now, personal computers are no longer the wave of the future. So what is? Tablet computers—iPads? Perhaps it's time to recycle this technology, and who might assist us in accomplishing this? Boomers!

Now, I have greatly abbreviated this story, but the point worth noting is that this program was created by listening, rather than telling Boomers what we want them do. We live in an age of great discovery that Boomers helped to create. With an attentive ear, they can help the church fashion a bright and innovative future.

CIRCLES ("CIRCLE OF FRIENDS")

Another Boomer-initiated effort was a program designed for young adults with developmental disabilities. One of my parishioners, Dennis, had spent most of his adult career employed by a large center outside Chicago that worked with adults who had developmental disabilities. During this time he became more and more concerned that the program designed to support these individuals and their families isolated them from the mainstream population. His passion was to find ways in which they could contribute, and directly participate in, mainstream society. The established structure provided support for these individuals and their families to the point of their high school graduation, but after that their options radically declined. "Could the church," Dennis wondered, "create something that might fill this need or gap?"

What developed was a program named Circles (Circles of Friends) that partnered with area business leaders to uncover jobs and discover employers who were willing to become advocates for these young adults. They helped by identifying jobs in the public workplace, in contrast to the traditional, isolated workshops, where these young adults could be employed. It worked! In fact, one of the outcomes was that the congregation created a cleaning service that provided custodial services for a number of local businesses and churches. Volunteers negotiated the services and provided mentoring/oversight. Partnerships were created, where necessary, with licensed agencies, and an outreach was born that I never would have imagined a church to formulate. But then, when one thinks about it, what better, ready-made network of people, jobs, and ideas is there than the church?

Similarly, during the recent recession, a woman decided to use her interests and skills to establish a jobs board and network on the Internet. Need a job? Post it! Know of an employment opportunity? Post it! Aware of an individual or network that might be of assistance? Post it! What a simple, but wonderful idea.

CHARITABLE SUPPORT

Initiated, created, and funded by a Boomer couple related to our church, the Manning Arts gallery seeks to blend skills and passions in an effort to provide financial support for charities. What Sean and Laura have done is use their gallery as a vehicle for the creation of artwork, with the subsequent donation of any sales going to the church and other local charities. The gallery can be visited in person or online. Artwork can be purchased by anyone, anywhere, anytime, electronically. Youth groups spend evenings creating their own paintings or clay works that can be marketed. If the artwork is sold, a percentage is immediately returned to the designated charity, with a small percentage being retained for ongoing materials and general expenses.

This, like the other projects mentioned, so clearly illustrates those characteristics of passion, creativity, and innovation that we have previously identified with Boomers. Still in its initial stages, we have great hopes for this last effort. To learn more, visit themanningarts.org. Once there, search the site for "UCC/Faithloop" and look at the paintings created specifically for the benefit of the 2011 General Synod of the United Church of Christ.

SUPPORT COMMUNITY ENDEAVORS

Boomers are about their community as much as, and in many cases more than, they are their church. They often know more about "outside" community causes than they do their own congregation's endeavors, especially those with denominational ties. And the church that raises awareness and participates in these community efforts will find broader recognition and support from this generation. Probably the best "old school" example of doing this is leading a food or clothing drive for a local agency. But walk/runs for breast cancer, golf tournaments for children with heart disease, and book drives for homeless shelters are more in tune with Boomers. Advertise local events of specific interest in your church and list how people can get involved. Show that your church cares, not just about itself, but about the broader community. Energy spent outside the church does not subtract from, but adds to, energy inside the church. And don't forget, if any outside cause you support prints a pamphlet or shirt as advertising for their event, include your QR code.

PARTNERSHIPS

I have already mentioned a number of programs that our church has been involved with that could never have taken place without being connected to outside organizations. Never discard an idea because of a lack of knowledge or funding. Grants, scholarships, and gifts are always available if the cause is right. One of the best connections I have experienced was with the Good Shepherd Hospital in Barrington, Illinois. They not only had a commitment to reaching the broader community, they had funding and staff allocated to achieve this. Working with them, our church was able to accomplish a number of projects.

In this time of financial constriction, everyone is looking for better, more efficient ways to succeed. Whether collaborating with a business, community group, or nearby church, seek ways to augment funds and multiply volunteers. Instead of thinking *big*, think *broad*. Business has learned the benefits of outsourcing, and our churches could benefit by outreach outsourcing. The more the merrier, and the greater the possibilities.

TECHIES

Consider gathering not just the professionals but also the hobbyists in your congregation who love technology in order to assist the church or help educate others who may be intimidated by computers or the Internet. Use their skills to manage electronic publications as well as implement web, text, and Twitter tools. Encourage and resource them for one-on-one or group learning times where others are taught the "ins and outs" of the web or their computer, smartphone, or iPad. People can't use the resources your church provides online if they don't know how. They can't go to the church's Facebook page if they are intimidated by the notion of setting up their own Facebook page.

An older gentleman courageously made the leap into the smartphone world, only to find that his battery kept dying quicker and quicker. Taking it to a service provider, he was told that he never shut off the "applications" he had opened, so they were continually running in the background, draining his battery. When these were closed, and a few other modifications made, his phone worked perfectly. In fact, he suddenly received responses to about one hundred e-mail messages that he thought he had sent over the past year. All of a sudden, any number of relatives were glad to hear he was coming to visit them. The only problem was, he already had!

Involve those who are already passionate about technology to share their knowledge and enthusiasm with others. You will be surprised where it might lead and who might help.

ADOPT A HIGHWAY, PARK, OR BEACH

Selecting a specific area to beautify and keep clean of trash resonates with Boomers' love for the environment. Dates can be regularly scheduled. The purpose and outcome are clear. Families can participate. Fellowship occurs. As an added benefit, the caretaker group is given a sign with its organization's name on it. Win! Win! Win!

COMPASSION AND CARE

Stephen Ministry (see www.stephenministries.org) continues to be a worthwhile and attractive ministry for the Boomer age group, offering the training and oversight needed to supplement what many seek—the chance to do pastoral care. My suggestion is that you broaden this model to apply other skills that individuals may possess and match their lifestyles. Are their members who need rides to their physician? Do spouses caring for a husband or wife need a break? Is there an elderly person who could use some help with cleaning or "handyman" tasks? Can someone answer general questions about car, plumbing, or electrical issues? Is there a need not just to collect but also to deliver food items to the local pantry? Any nurses? Establish a Sunday where they take blood pressures after church (for more how-to information, Google search "parish nursing"). Create a volunteer group/list that can easily be accessed and coordinated. Help people to help people. Put to work the resources already at hand.

ARTISTS OF THE SPIRIT

Just as there are individuals with technological skills and knowledge, almost every church has individuals with interests and abilities in various arts. Do you have people who love to act? Find resources and opportunities for them to share in worship. Do you have individuals who love to cook? Italian! Mexican! Cajun! Have a day where they share their talents. (Better yet, have them do so in a way that the food can be delivered to a homeless shelter.) Are there people who love to quilt and sew? Maybe they would like to teach younger members. Perhaps they could make (as one group in our church did) quilts for infants at the local children's hospital.

We have a number of artists in our congregation who have upon occasion presented an art show. Out of this we discovered a woman who was willing to paint an entire hallway of our church's education wing with a mural depicting Noah's ark. Along these same lines, a quilter was asked if she would consider making a series of seasonal altar cloths for our sanctuary. She did, and we greatly enjoy them throughout the year. (See page 121 in the "Resources" section.)

Use your spiritual gifts inventory to name and claim the talents and passions of those in your midst. Those invited to participate will benefit, and so will God's ministry.

CHILDREN! CHILDREN! CHILDREN!

Boomers are about children! They will always have a big place in their hearts for anything related to children. So here are some ideas to explore:

In the fall, implement a "back-to-school" backpack effort. Invite people to purchase a backpack and fill it with the supplies needed for a child to begin school. (Often local school supply stores such as Staples have lists of required supplies for each grade level at local schools.)

In the winter, start a coat collection for children in need.

Sponsor a "trunk-or-treat" community event at Halloween for your neighborhood using the church parking lot. Members decorate their cars and pass out treats for children in the neighborhood. So the kids and their parents go car to car rather than door to door. A number of churches I spoke with have had great success doing this. Another church, the First United Methodist Church in Scottsbluff, Nebraska, had members who, in conjunction with trunk-or-treat, built a hay bale maze on the church grounds that the families could walk through.

Create a tutoring program or an after-school arts or music activity. Invite your retired teachers to continue using their years of experience in a different way.

See if you have an individual who can teach classes for parents on budgeting or financial planning.

Invite retiring health-care professionals to share their knowledge (about diet, exercise, and common illnesses such as diabetes) in ways they find meaningful and manageable.

Create partnerships between those who have raised children (Boomers) and younger parents. In many churches, "adopt-a-grandparent" programs have created great connections between generations. Perhaps this is another way to lend support and pass the wisdom of experience from generation to generation.

15

Faith and Fun

Over the years, I have raced cars (which I loved), flown in "kit" planes (that never should have gotten off the ground), sat through operas (which I really did not enjoy), and attended performances by aging "rock stars" (who long ago should have "rolled" into retirement) as a way of knowing and enjoying the people around whom I live and with whom I hope to someday retire.

Spending time with people in areas where they are comfortable creates the corridors for connection that are critical for bringing them closer to any church. This is why fun activities are so important for ministry aimed at Boomers. They want to have fun. In the midst of all the serious stuff the church tries to do, never underestimate the value of having a good time—the first half of "good news!"

PASS-A-GRILLE-GAMES

This series of events is based on the old college intramural model, and it has been highly successful in reaching the Boomer age bracket at our church. What we have done is schedule four or five physical activities (team events) over the course of five months. These vary, so age or general skills are not significant. Team "fans" are factored into the final scoring, so everyone can feel a part of a team. There is a sense of competition, but the focus is on fellowship and fun. The specific activities involved were:

- softball—After several years we switched this to kickball in response to the expressed desire to be more inclusive of young children and older adults.

- horseshoes—a great activity for all ages.
- Jingle Bell Jog (December)—a community "walk/run" charity along the waterfront in St. Petersburg. Families bring children in wagons and dogs on leashes and enjoy participating in this citywide event. Afterward, participants gather at a motorhome for refreshments, hot chocolate, and laughter.
- tennis and bowling (alternating between the two)—Bowling was great but the venue limiting for observers. Bowling alleys are also very noisy, a hindrance for fellowship. Tennis provided good participation, but managing skill levels was difficult.
- shuffleboard—A big hit! Cap this off with a chili cooking contest and you have a real winner! Many activities might be used to replicate this program (frisbee golf, bocce ball), depending upon the make-up and geographic location of your congregation. What's important is to be aware of the public or private facilities available for use and sensitive to your participants' needs/abilities (in other words, be inclusive).

CIGS (COMMON INTEREST GROUPS)

People love to share their personal interests with others, so why not create relationships around these things. Introduce two fishermen and you'll have ten stories. Have a Sunday for motorcycle enthusiasts and you'll have a party. Walkers? Runners? Bicyclists? Bring them together.[1] Build upon passions people already possess, and in time add some new ones. If they are reluctant to join a "church group," create a group or gathering that is less threatening. At all levels of church, relationship-building is a foundation for long-term success. Uncover those things that are already a part of people's lives and then *connect the dots!* Never underestimate one-time events, especially if they provide an opportunity for visitors to participate. In Florida, we are keenly aware that many of today's drop-ins are tomorrow's permanent retiree residents (this would be a great way to use Pinterest on your web page).

FAN FUN

One event that was a lot of fun revolved around a Sunday in which we invited worship attendees to wear their favorite college or alma mater's colors (sweatshirts, jerseys, etc.). We scheduled this at the beginning of the college football season because it is a big event in our area. We decorated our fellowship hall with school banners and pennants. We provided appropriately decorated refreshments. People with Big Ten or SEC connections, as well as affiliations to multiple other conferences, had their designated spaces to meet and greet each other. Members and strangers alike made new friends. It was energizing! It was fun! (A variation might be celebrating each month's birthdays during the fellowship time following worship.)

MOVIE NIGHTS

Not a new idea, but still a good one. We have never done this as many churches do, monthly, but in a brief series. That is, one Advent we showed childhood Christmas movies from the 1950s or '60s (*White Christmas, It's a Wonderful Life, A Charlie Brown Christmas*). During Lent we held a "Jesus in the Movies" series (*Jesus of Toronto, The Last Temptation of Christ, Jesus Christ Superstar*). A supplemental text for this series is W. Barnes Tatum's book by the same name.[2] Another suggestion might be the *Lord of the Rings Trilogy*, with the accompanying book, *The Lord of the Rings and Philosophy*.[3] Whether showing an older movie or going to a current movie, this is a form of fellowship that many enjoy.

The key is uncovering and then using those common points of interest already present in culture through which people allow you to connect their lives. At any time we are offered a number of wonderful opportunities, if only we would take advantage of them. Dan Brown's novel *The Da Vinci Code* intrigued millions of people. What a wonderful opportunity to show the movie and have a discussion about the formation of the church and the Gospels. Or how about the recent productions by National Geographic or the Discovery Channel, *The Gospel of Thomas* or *Mysteries of the Bible*? People are watching these already. Why not create events that use them to your advantage? (A good resource to consult for ideas and materals is www.thethoughtfulchristian.com.)

COFFEE SHOPS

Remember the popularity of a Friday night in college, at a local coffee shop with a performing artist? Use the performing artists in your area or church, and have an evening of music at church or under a member's gazebo. Jazz, folk, whatever—the coffee shop setting worked back then and still can today. Attend a high school, college, or professional event. Visit a local art gallery or museum. Schedule a church trip to view a local exhibit, or take in a musical or play. The bus ride alone builds new relationships. Our church has provided a number of concerts during the program year, including performances by Ed Kilbourne (www.edkilbourne.com), who epitomizes the coffee house style.

GAME NIGHTS

Favorite board games are set up at tables in the church's fellowship hall. Individuals start at specific tables and then, after a set period of time, rotate to the spot of another player. It's fun. It mixes people together. It provides interaction. For example, how about an intergenerational night of Christmas Pictionary:

Divide the group into teams. Each team sends one person up to the leader, who gives them the name of a Christmas-related object or carol. Then the person returns to his or her group and in the manner of Pictionary tries to get the group to guess the name of the carol/object by drawing only (no verbal cues or pantomimes).

As soon as the group knows the answer, they must as a group sing it if it is a song or shout it out if it is an object until the leader gives the okay. Use songs like "Jingle Bells," "Deck the Halls," "Angels We Have Heard on High," "Away in a Manger," "Silent Night," . . . You get the picture.)

SOCIAL CIRCLES

One church funneled newcomers into "Fellowship Circles" that were carefully designed to match people of similar interests and ages. They met monthly for an event of their own choosing. Groups were initially committed for a nine-month period; however, some lasted for years. This effort did require a staff person, or very committed volunteer, to work with clergy to identify and assimilate members with common interests, into groups. A variation that many congregations use is "Dinners for Eight." This is a one-time mixer aimed at accomplishing the same thing. Eight participants are matched and invited to gather, either for one or two meals, at locations of their choice.

Over the years, one the most successful things my wife and I have done is host social gatherings at our home. We love our annual Epiphany Party, which is casual and solely intended to build relationships within the church that might otherwise not transpire. These are well worth our time and resources—or those of the church.

NAME TAGS

Most every church has name tags these days. Ours, however, not only reveal the name of the wearer, but also include the person's state of origin and/or birth. This is especially fun in Florida where nearly everybody is from somewhere else. People make instant connections and immediate conversations. If it works for Disney, it can work for us. Simple, but effective.

RETREATS

Weekend retreats are still very effective, especially if centered around themes, gender issues, and the like. One of our goals is to hold an intergenerational camping trip at a local state park. We will organize various group activities, but also allow for people to walk, talk, and sit together around the campfire. There are few things in life more bonding than time around a campfire.

SPECIAL EVENTS

Small town or large city; country church or downtown setting, there are events and activities near you. Take advantage of them, as a church group. Here are a few suggestions:

- Go to a mystery playhouse (near to us is a Murder Mystery Train ride).

- Organize a paddle boat dinner/dance jazz cruise (if you live near a bay, lake, river, or other body of water).

- One church sponsored a private railcar train ride into Chicago for a little Christmas shopping, along with "Skate on State Street" and dinner in the Walnut Room at Macy's.

- Attend a concert (such as at Fiddler's Green, outside Boston; Ravinia, north of Chicago; or Red Rocks, west of Denver).

- Organize a hot air champagne breakfast, balloon ride.

- Take in a local sporting event, whether high school or professional; this can be a fun event built upon our culture's love of sports. (Go, Tampa Bay Rays!)

Bring people together to enjoy an event and each other's company. It will bear fruit.

16

WINDOWS OF RECEPTIVITY

I use this title because I have discovered over the years that there are natural times of transition in life when people are more receptive to new ideas and outside influences. There are points in life where people more readily turn to others for guidance and assistance. For instance, it is commonly recognized that youth drift from church following high school, returning briefly for marriage. But this all changes as they mature in their jobs and lifestyle, finally settling down after the birth of a child. It is then that many touch base again with the church. And they will continue to seek assistance and advice at identifiable stages of their children's development (early childhood; starting grade school, middle school, and high school; and at various stages of adolescence).

Recognizing these stages, churches have provided day care, preschool, after-school, and multiple youth-oriented programs for years. What I am suggesting is that the same theory be applied to Boomers as they reach toward a new stage and final phase in their lives—retirement. Like the earlier stages of their lives, this is a "window of receptivity" that revolves around newness, uncertainty, and basic personal needs. So the questions are: What points of access into their lives is the church now afforded that weren't available several years ago? What are the needs of Boomers at this particular point of transition? What programs do we offer that meet these needs and build a bridge for this transition?

PARENTAL CARE

Of increasing concern for Boomers is caring for their aging parents, especially as they often find themselves hundreds of miles and several states away. This is a matter of constant concern for churches in Florida, given our high retiree population. In some ways we are prepared, and in others not, as we are often asked to build a bridge of support between a child living in Ohio and the parent(s) near us. Following are some strategies we have discovered that are helpful.

Contact person. Recruit an identifiable person (perhaps staff, but more likely a volunteer) who is regularly in contact with the parent and can provide objective information to the child regarding the parent's health and well-being. A Stephen Ministry program can be of great assistance in this regard; however, it need not be this formal. It may just be someone who plays the role of the concerned neighbor. In Florida, our older members already perform this task for one another, so it's really a matter of teaching them how they can appropriately help by reporting to a staff person or designated church volunteer.

Contact list. Create a contact list of family members to be notified when a particular event or change occurs with their parents, and keep it on file at the church. You might also make a file available for keeping living wills and memorial arrangements, which can then be provided to the family or the care-giving child.

Caregiver/facility listing. An available publication or a web page that lists residential homes and services in the area can be extremely useful to visiting children of elders. Speaking firsthand, it is hard to assist one's parent when you do not know the community and may only be able to visit for a short time. What facilities are available for assisted living? Nursing care? Alzheimer's care? Have staff/clergy personally visited these facilities, talked with directors, and taken a tour of the facilities?

Service listing. Keep a list of legal and medical services available in your area and specific to your state, perhaps including classes or seminars on topics such as dementia, Parkinson's, Medicare, funeral arrangements, and what assisted living entails. When someone knocks on your minister's office door and inquires as to health-care services or physicians, what honest recommendations or advice can the minister give? Wills, medical power of attorney, and so forth vary from state to state, and it has been my experience that children caring for their parents are not well advised as to what needs to be in place in order to make decisions at very critical times.

Personal support. This is important not just for the aging parent, but also for the caring child. Certainly offer one-on-one counseling when possible, but maybe also offer support through small groups. Such groups can be quite informal, bringing together individuals who are going through similar care-giving struggles. As if dealing with a parent whose body or mind is failing isn't difficult enough, traversing the legal and medical system can be a nightmare. And when the time comes to relocate a "mom" or "dad" into a nursing care facility, the personal guilt and loss, often complicated by sibling/family issues, can be overwhelming. Speaking from personal experience, just having someone to think, cry, pray, and maybe laugh . . . even just a little . . . with you through the decisions and challenges of this time can be a real lifesaver.

Physical assistance equipment room. We maintain a room in our church where we store equipment that might be needed for those who are aging (wheelchairs, walkers, crutches, canes, and the like). We have found that these items may be provided by various health-care services, but in some cases are not. Even if they are only used for temporary assistance, such as assisting in bringing a parent to church, these donated tools for care are greatly appreciated.

LEARNING EVENTS REGARDING FINANCES AND RETIREMENT

Boomers want to retire. It is the promised land they have been laboring toward for years. Not that previous generations didn't, but Boomers have made this their "holy grail." Yet for many it appears farther and farther away. They are thus very interested in understanding how to better align their finances with their goals and dreams. This is especially applicable to later Boomers (born 1956–1964) who are looking toward retirement with a much longer horizon.

Now, the church is not in the business of financial planning, but we are in the business of stewardship, which is about "all of life." Any way we can help people live healthier, better, and more secure lives is one more way to better our society, as well as our churches. Changes are continually being made in regard to Social Security, Medicare, and income taxes. These are always subjects of interest around which forums can be offered. Find ways to be informed, and then to inform.

REHIREMENT?

This particular need is driven by retirees' desire to continue contributing to society in a meaningful and fulfilling way and, often, the basic need to augment one's income. In both cases, Boomers are not looking to be fully "retired," but what we might call "rehired" in either a paying or volunteer capacity, perhaps doing something entirely different, and, in many cases, what they may have desired for a lifetime. In this regard, Marc Freedman writes:

> Rejecting phased retirement, Boomers are looking forward to this next phase of work as a destination, not a way-station between the end of midlife work and the beginning of full-on retirement. Instead of phasing out they are focusing in, attempting to find more from work, not less: more flexibility, to be sure, but equally more meaning and greater impact.[1]

A 2005 study done by MetLife Foundation/Civic Ventures New Face of Work reveals that a good number of people between the ages of fifty and seventy have a strong desire to find work that they consider meaningful. Consider how many individuals have left the private sector to attend seminary and become ordained clergy over the last twenty or thirty years. The challenge, and first step, is to define what "work" actually means in these years. In this regard, Phil Burgess provides a starting point through what he calls the "five categories of work" in retirement:

- Paid work. Many retirees seek an opportunity to continue working for a fee or salary; many are quite capable of transferring their professional skills into consulting positions.

- In-kind work. People might offer some kind of service, say, accounting, in return for car or yard care. This might include working as an usher at a game or concert venue in return for tickets.

- Volunteer work. This includes creating crafts, donating time to community organizations, hospitals, and so on.

- Samaritan work. This is person-to-person care-giving or assistance arranged informally.

- Enrichment work. Examples would include working with photography, computers, or other languages, or doing philanthropy.[2]

Retirement offers the wonderful gift of time; the challenge is determining how and where to appropriately use, but not *overuse* it, because there are so many opportunities and requests. Perhaps this is where the church can lend a hand. What are some ways this might be accomplished?

- Bring together Boomers who are interested in preparing for this third stage of life to share thoughts, goals, hopes, and possible connections. The church is a networking dream; use it to discover, uncover, and introduce.

- Create a "jobs" bulletin board, on your website, where those seeking potential employees with particular skills can post their openings. This could be an especially beneficial way to connect not-for-profit agencies with individuals who are motivated but otherwise might be overqualified and unaffordable.

- Use the spiritual gifts inventory or values assessment mentioned earlier to identify areas of skill/interest for those seeking alternative forms of employment.

- Make available books on this subject (see additional resources). Better yet, form some discussions around the insights and suggestions of the authors of these books.

- Promote an event where a jobs professional (perhaps specifically skilled with this age group) talks about opportunities or offers an interest inventory that might assist in helping folks plan a course for their future

TARGETED PASTORAL ATTENTION

Quoting from the Holmes-Rahe Stress Scale, Charles Arn lists the top forty stress events for individuals age fifty and over. They range from the obvious—divorce or death of a spouse—to the genesis of minor physical problems and from medical insurance issues to the remarriage of a parent. Some seem a bit trivial, while others are very critical. In either case, they are clues for increased pastoral care and potential. Arn notes the implementation of a Crisis Deployment Team in one particular church where, "member-to-member," a tangible expression of presence and care was shared with people caught in these situations.[3]

In the last church I served, there were a number of airline pilots for whom retirement was a particularly stressful time. For years, the nonpilot spouse had learned to live "solo" while the other traveled. Suddenly this person who had seemed to never be around was always hanging around. It presented a significant adjustment. My church overlooked this window of receptivity by not providing any kind of formal support to match what should have been an obvious need. There were groups in the community, however, that did. Opportunity missed!

Finally, I don't think we can underestimate the impact of health changes for this generation. So motivated by activity, any change in expected physical ability can have a severe mental/emotional impact. I speak from personal experience—I was recently diagnosed with a rare malady, chronic inflammatory demyelinating polyneuropathy (CIDP), the outcome of which is unpredictable. What I do foresee is that, in some form or another, it will be physically limiting. Dreams, hopes, and goals for the third stage of my life all changed in the moment when that diagnosis was pronounced. I instantly felt different—separated from my peers.

I am not sure what shape a formal response in matters such as these should take; however, I do know that care in these instances of transition are critical for reaching and keeping people in touch and involved with the church.

17

FINISHING STRONG! FINAL THOUGHTS

ow do we then summarize all we have touched on throughout
this book regarding reaching Baby Boomers in our ministry
as they move toward retirement? Well, one particular biblical
narrative comes to mind for me, that of Solomon. A *wunderkind* of
ancient Israel, Solomon is remembered and admired for his judi-
ciousness and will be eternally revered as the builder of the Jerusalem
Temple. Aside from David, he is celebrated as the greatest of Israel's
kings. The tragedy of Solomon's story is that his greatness came at a
horrific price.

Asking of God only wisdom at the beginning of his rule (1
Kings 3:7–9), Solomon modeled the ideal head of state. But by the
time his reign ended, things were very different. He had built a
spectacular place of worship that would be associated with his name
forever, but its magnificence was dwarfed by the extravagance of
his personal palace. What a contrast that the temple required seven
years to build while his home demanded thirteen (1 Kings 6:37–
7:1). And yes, Israel reached its peak under his reign, but at a great
cost, including the enslavement of his own people. My point?
Solomon succeeded in many ways, but failed in the most important.
He lost his sense of "true north." He lost touch with his calling for
life. He started strong, but finished weak!

To understand Boomers is to recognize that they have no intention of making the same mistake. Like Solomon, many have accomplished much. They have succeeded in business. They have
traveled, learned, and done incredible things. But they have no in-

tention of fading away in their last phase of life. They will do more! They fully intend to finish strong. How? Many are unsure, but the desire for inward growth and its outward application is very, very real, of this I am sure. So . . .

EMBRACE RISK!

Don't let your church die because you suffer from a risk aversion! In the anthology *Communication and Change in American Religious History,* Leonard Sweet posits that one of the main reasons for the explosion of evangelical Christianity on the American frontier was the adaption of printed material, primarily the pamphlet. Now, this communication tool may seem obvious today, but at the time it was revolutionary. And to Sweet's point, the pamphlet became a major vehicle for reaching the American frontier that most of the European rooted church traditions "pooh-poohed." Add to that the "go-to-them, out-there" work of the circuit riders, and you have the seeds of a growth story, the results of which are still evident today.

> Prior to the nineteenth century, books preserved beliefs and knowledge rather than disseminating new information or retailing opinion. Knowledge transmission by print rather than oral means brought with it the privatization and democratization of knowledge. The individual accessed knowledge without need of family or friends or employers and accessed it at will.[1]

Many of the ideas that have been suggested in this book probably feel "different" or maybe even "ridiculous"; however, the church that will fail with the Baby Boomer generation is the church that is unwilling to *risk failing.* It required nearly six years of trial and error with our alternative worship service until we felt that we were starting to get it right. Style, time, flow—all these were things that had to be personally experienced before they could be tailored to local needs. Most of us, that is, clergy in the mainline tradition, do very well what we have been trained to do. The problem is, as for classical music, the audience that our traditional style reaches is shrinking.

What's to replace it? Well, that's the challenge before us. So don't "take care," as we are so fond of saying, but rather "take a risk!"

THINK PEOPLE TO PEOPLE

If Boomers have invented a world about "them," then it is from the inside out, not the outside in, that our thinking must begin—but not end. Whether preaching, teaching, or leading a discussion on world hunger, it's not the macro but the micro that needs to be addressed first—how does it impact "me"? How does it relate to "my" life? And then, in what way does it apply to others' lives and to our world?

In the course of a recent sermon, I asked our congregation to take out of their wallets or purses a five-dollar bill. "I'm going to perform a magic trick," I told them. "That is, I'm going to make this five-dollar bill change before your eyes.

"Look at it," I urged, "and tell me what five dollars will or won't buy. I know it won't buy a meal at McDonald's or Chick-fil-A. I know that it won't even get you two gallons worth of gas. And at Starbucks, it will only buy you a peppermint mocha, if you settle for a tall, the smallest size. But if you Google-search world hunger, as it relates to children around the world, you'll find that same five dollars will feed a child for anywhere from one to twenty days. Look at that five-dollar bill again; it just changed in what it can do—what it represents—right before your eyes."

Whether talking about wounded veterans returning from Afghanistan, friends who have openly shared their sexual orientation, or hunger around the world, the more a personal face is put on an issue, the more passionate Boomers become. And the more face-to-face their connection, the greater their desire to overcome and change the world.

> Christians first must unlearn an understanding of the church in which the word coffee is often only another expression for the word fellowship. Church is not an organization you join, but an organism of which you are a living member, attached to other members of the organism as

surely as the five people in mountaineering are attached to the same rope. You may scrape against one another, get tangled up in troubles of someone else's making, get vexed at the dirt someone kicks your way, or even come not to like some of the other climbers. But beyond those feelings lies the awareness that together you constitute what the Germans call a *Schickalsgemeinde*, a "fate community" that rises or falls together. You share a common destiny.[2]

It's about relationships—small groups—community. Being the body of Christ.

KEEP IT BRIEF, IMPORTANT, AND GRATIFYING

Remember, Boomers favor specific tasks with broad implications and personally satisfying results. I don't think we can underestimate the negatives of meetings that involve a lot of time with less than satisfying conclusions. Why is it that Boomers in my church are more than willing to dedicate time to hospice or a homeless shelter than to other church groups or committees? Because the task is specific, the outcomes apparent, and the gratification nearly immediate. Where Boomers get involved, and passionately so, is where there are tangible expectations and results that match and contribute to higher ideals.

I love a story relayed by Elizabeth Jeffries regarding an afternoon walk in the village of Sturbridge, Massachusetts. There, between presentations at a conference, she happened to walk into a store named the Hour Glass. She states how all around her were clocks—table clocks, grandfather and grandmother clocks, mantel clocks, even alarm clocks. It was while enthusiastically absorbing all these clocks that an elderly and rather frail gentleman in his eighties walked in. She recalls, "He wore a pinstriped shirt with sleeves rolled up, wide navy suspenders, and bifocals with a jeweler's loop off to the side. Mainly he wore a loving, gentle face with lots of life lines and a big warm smile!" Assuming he was the clock repair person, she said, "These are magnificent! You must repair these clocks, right?" The elderly man paused, thought for a moment, smiled at her apparent naiveté, and then replied, "Oh no, my dear. I don't repair clocks. I restore history!"[3]

That is how Boomers want to view their contributions in time, and beyond their time. They wish to give, but in ways that are deeply meaningful and lasting. Maybe they won't restore history, but they're still committed to making history. Nothing wrong with that!

LISTEN! LISTEN! LISTEN!

Creating church that's relevant and innovative involves pastors and leaders who are *in touch* with Boomers, both within and outside of their church. Skeptical of institutions most of their lives, Boomers are not going to flock to our doors simply because their life's journey may be winding toward its conclusion. Besides, they don't really believe their journey will end any time soon! Therefore, involving them in the church begins with being involved in their lives. Spend time with them. Get to know their passions and you will discover ways for those passions to breathe life into your church.

Boomers are unconventional, but not faithless; noninstitutional, but not uninterested. Listen! Partner! The Boomer generation has much to offer, and there is only one real reason our churches can't be recipients—*us!*

BE FLEXIBLE, BE RELEVANT, BE INCLUSIVE

I was once fortunate to observe a little girl as she played with a Lego train. The toy was such that it was up to her to establish the course of the track, place the train upon it, and drive. Now, if I were doing this, I would first put the track together in the form of an oval. Then I would place the train upon it and push it around. This is not what the five-year-old girl did. Rather, she put together a small portion of track, immediately placed the train upon it, and began to push.

What was she going to do, I wondered, when her train reached the end of the track? Simple—she merely picked up some pieces from behind the train and attached them to the track in front of the train, and it went on. It wasn't important that her track formed an oval. Nor was it important to her that the track was established in a preconceived form. Instead, she allowed herself the freedom to find her way, even if moving ahead entailed bending first this way, then that.

The "curse" of the church is its interpretation of the word "tradition." That is, if we do anything once, whether a choir concert or chili cook-off, especially if it reaps any kind of success, it suddenly becomes an annual event. And it stays that way until either it dies or we do. Please don't misunderstand; we need tradition lest we "throw the baby out with the bathwater." But included in our definition of this word must be the idea of constantly laboring to interpret and share God's word in ways that help it to remain alive and vital. Walt Disney once said, "Disneyland will never be completed, as long as there is imagination left in the world."[4] Can we say the same thing about God's Spirit and our churches? In far too many instances, probably not.

Some things must die before others can be born. There are such things in life as necessary losses. If you can't get volunteers any more, maybe it's not the volunteers that are the problem, but the tasks we are inviting them to perform. In the time it has taken for you to read this book, the world has changed dramatically. This *is* the new tradition, and it's not all bad. Flannery O'Connor defined fiction as "mystery that is lived"; perhaps we would do well to accept this as a model for ministry as well.[5]

In a perfect world, our churches would implement many of the ideas talked about in this book, but in reality we won't, because we can't. But if we can take several and do them better, focusing on the strengths and needs that uniquely belong to our congregations, our efforts will bear fruit. Likewise, some of the conclusions I have reached may not apply to your setting, but the point that cannot be missed is that our society is aging, and our churches along with it.

But at the same time, if we give some attention to Boomers, we have the opportunity to grow younger. Of this, I am convinced! In this, there is cause to rejoice. Once upon a time, our mainline churches missed the Boomer generation. As they come around a second time, moving toward the final stage of their lives, we have the opportunity to write an alternative ending to that story. And I choose to believe that, like them, we too can finish strong! The fun has just begun.

> We were ring-around-the-rosy children.
> They were circles around the sun.
> Never give up, never slow down.
> Never grow old, never ever die young.
>
> —*James Taylor, "Never Die Young," 1988*

NOTES

INTRODUCTION

1. Julie Sullivan, "Baby Boomers, who drove the cultural shift to SUVs and consumerism, now driving the shift to public transit and yoga," OregonLive, May 10, 2011, www.Oregonlive.com/health /index.ssf/2011/05/baby_boomers_drive_the_cultura.html.

2. Matilda White Riley, quoted in Marc Freedman, *Prime Time—How Baby Boomers Will Revolutionize Retirement and Transform America* (New York: Public Affairs, 1999), 22.

3. Mike Perrault and Keith Matheny, "As Golf Declines, Life on the Links Ain't What It Used to Be," *USA Today,* January 16, 2012, www.usatoday.com/money/economy/housing/story/2012-01-15/golf-communities-real-estate/52591988/1.

4. Freedman, *Prime Time,* 22.

5. Daniel Boorstin, quoted in Freedman, *Prime Time,* 22.

6. Mark Twain *Life on the Mississippi Complete,* (Project Gutenberg EBook #245, 2006), 398, www.gutenberg.org/files/245/245-h/245-h.htm.

CHAPTER 1

1. Phyllis Moen, "Midcourse: Navigating Retirement and a New Life Stage," synopsis at www.encore.org/find/resources/fact-sheet-older, from Jeylan Mortimer and Michael J. Shanahan, eds., *Handbook of the Life Course* (New York: Kluwer Publishers, 2003), 274.

CHAPTER 2

1. Bill Pennington, "Baby Boomers Stay Active and So Do Their Doctors," *The New York Times,* April 16, 2006, www.nytimes.com /2006/04/16/sports/16boomers.html?_r=1&pagewanted=all.

2. "Global Health Club Industry Surpasses 128 Million Members—The 2011 IHRSA Global Report Details Industry Growth," May 26, 2011, www.ihrsa.org/media-center/2011/5/26/global-health-club-industry-surpasses-128-million-members-th.html.

3. Frank Litsky, "Cowher Resigns, Stops Short of Retiring," *The New York Times,* Jan. 6, 2007, www.nytimes.com/2007/01/06/sports /football/06cowher.html.

4. Tom Petty, "Mary Jane's Last Dance," *Anthology—Through the Years,* Universal Music, 2000.

5. J. Walker Smith and Ann Clurman, *Generation Ageless: How Baby Boomers Are Changing the Way We Live Today . . . and They're Just Getting Started* (New York: Collins Press, 2007), 63.

CHAPTER 3

1. J. Walker Smith and Ann Clurman, *Generation Ageless: How Baby Boomers Are Changing the Way We Live Today . . . and They're Just Getting Started* (New York: Collins Press, 2007), 83.

2. D'Vera Cohn and Paul Taylor, "Baby Boomers Approach 65—Glumly," Pew Research Center, December 20, 2010, www.pewsocial trends.org/2010/12/20/baby-boomers-approach-65-glumly/.

3. Smith and Clurman, *Generation Ageless*, 35.

4. ABC Nightly News, August 11, 2011.

5. David Crary, "Boomers Will Be Pumping Billions into Anti-Aging Industry," Huffington Post, August 20, 2011, www.huffington post.com/2011/08/20/boomers-anti-aging-industry_n_932109.html.

6. Smith and Clurman, *Generation Ageless,* 25.

CHAPTER 4

1. Heidi Mitchell, "A Whole Other Ball Game," *The Wall Street Journal,* Jan. 28, 2012, online.wsj.com/article/SB1000142405297 0204616504577172962733647798.html.

2. Focalyst, "Baby Boomers 'Not-So-Me Generation,'" Boomer Cafe, Sept. 22, 2008, www.boomercafe.com/2008/09/22/baby-boomers -'not-so-me-generation'/.

3. Joanne Fritz, "Tapping the Volunteer Power of Baby Boomers," About.com, nonprofit.about.com/od/volunteers/a/boomervolunteer .htm, accessed July 31, 2012.

4. Edward Piegza, "New Survey Shows Baby Boomers Seeking Active Adventure Travel," posted January 21, 2011, www.classic

journeys.com/blog/new/surveys-show-baby-boomers-seeking
-active-adventure-travel/.

   5. Amy Hanson, *Baby Boomers and Beyond: Tapping the Ministry Talents and Passions of Adults over 50* (San Francisco: Jossey-Bass, 2010), 28.

CHAPTER 5

   1. Walter Isaacson, *Steve Jobs* (New York: Simon and Schuster, 2011), 178.

   2. Journey, "Don't Stop Believin,'" Sony Music, 2001.

   3. Harold Kushner, *Who Needs God* (New York: Summit Books, 1989), 188.

CHAPTER 6

   1. Pew Research Center, "The Generation Gap and the 2012 Election," November 3, 2011, www.people-press.org/2011/11/03/the-generation-gap-and-the-2012-election-3/.

   2. Jeffrey Love, "Political Behavior and Values across the Generations," *AARP* (July 2004), 10.

   3. Pew Research Center, "The Generation Gap and the 2012 Election," November 3, 2011, www.people-press.org/2011/11/03/the-generation-gap-and-the-2012-election-3/.

   4. J. Walker Smith and Ann Clurman, *Generation Ageless: How Baby Boomers Are Changing the Way We Live Today . . . and They're Just Getting Started* (New York: Collins Press, 2007), 120.

   5. Ibid., 128.

CHAPTER 7

   1. Walter Isaacson, *Steve Jobs* (New York: Simon and Schuster, 2011), 44.

   2. D'Vera Cohn and Paul Taylor, "Baby Boomers Approach 65—Glumly," Pew Research Center, December 20, 2010, www.pewsocialtrends.org/2010/12/20/baby-boomers-approach-65-glumly/, 5.

   3. Gary McIntosh, "Perspectives and Practices for Ministry with Baby Boomers," *Lifelong Faith* (Winter 2010), 37.

CHAPTER 8

1. Ron Lieber, "8 Reasons You Should Not Expect an Inheritence," *The New York Times,* June 21, 2008, www.nytimes.com/2008 /06/21/business/yourmoney/21money.html?_r=2&scp=1&sq=8%20 Reasons%20You%20Should%20Not%20Expect%20an%20Inheritance%20&st=cse.

2. Paul Taylor, "Baby Boomers Approach Age 60: From the Age of Aquarius to the Age of Responsibility," Pew Research Center, December 8, 2005, pewresearch.org/assets/social/pdf/socialtrends-boomers120805.pdf.

3. Richard H. Gentzler, Jr., *Aging and Ministry in the 21st Century* (Nashville: Discipleship Resources, 2008), 113.

CHAPTER 9

1. ABC News, "Inheritance and Wealth Transfer to Baby Boomers," December 27, 2010.

2. Michelle Slatalla, "Five Fascinating Philanthropists," *Barron's,* December 5, 2011, online.barrons.com/article/SB500014240527 48704854004577052601132573024.html#articleTabs_article%3D1.

3. Samuel G. Freedman, "Congregations Reeling from Decline in Donations," *The New York Times,* September 24, 2010, www.nytimes.com/2010/09/25/us/25religion.html?_r=1.

4. Leslie Scanlon, "Experts Say Churches Must Adapt to New Profile in Giving," The Presbyterian Outlook, December 15, 2011, www.pres-outlook.com/reports-a-resources3/presbyterian -heritage-articles3/11964-expert-says-churches-must-adapt-to-new -profile-of-charitable-giving.html.

5. Robert Powell, "Many of Us Won't Be Able to Retire Until Our 80s," *The Wall Street Journal,* June 9, 2011, articles.market watch.com/2011-06-09/finance/30766873_1_retirement-income-adequacy-aarp-report-employee-benefit-research-institute.

CHAPTER 10

1. Kathryn Zickuhr, "Generations 2010: Major Trends in Online Activities," Pew Internet and American Life Project, April 29–May

30, 2010, pewinternet.org/Reports/2010/Generations-2010/Trends.aspx?view=all.

CHAPTER 11

1. D'Vera Cohn and Paul Taylor, "Baby Boomers Approach 65—Glumly," Pew Research Center, December 20, 2010, www.pew socialtrends.org/2010/12/20/baby-boomers-approach-65-glumly/.

2. Marc Freedman Encore, *Finding Work that Matters in the Second Half of Life* (New York: Public Affairs, 2007), 9.

PART II

1. Josh Hammond and James Morrison, *The Stuff Americans Are Made Of* (New York: MacMillan, 1996), 1–2.

CHAPTER 12

1. Roy M. Oswald and Otto Kroeger, *Myers-Briggs Type Indicator; Personality Type and Religious Leadership* (Herndon, VA: Alban Institute, 1988).

2. Erik Rees, *S.H.A.P.E.: Finding and Fulfilling Your Unique Purpose for Life* (Grand Rapids: Zondervan, 2006), 2.

3. Rick Warren, *The Purpose Driven Life* (Grand Rapids: Zondervan, 2002), 171.

4. Rees, *S.H.A.P.E.*, 37.

5. Tom Rath, *Now, Discover Your Strengths* (New York: Simon and Schuster, 2001).

6. Kevin and Kay Brennfleck, *Live Your Calling* (San Francisco: Jossey-Bass, 2005).

7. Richard C. Morais, "The Age of Charity Clicks," Barron's: *Penta,* December 22, 2011, blogs.barrons.com/penta/2011/12/22/the-age-of-charity-clicks/.

8. Robert H. Schuller, *Your Church Has a Fantastic Future!* (Ventura, CA: Regal Books, 1986), 136.

CHAPTER 13

1. Leonard Sweet, *The Gospel According to Starbucks: Living with a Grande Passion* (Colorado Springs: Waterbook Press, 2007), 45–46.

2. Richard Saltus, "Losing Touch Reviving the Dying Art of Hands-on Medicine, *The Boston Globe,* June 7, 1999, www.highbeam .com/doc/1P2-8546764.html.

3. Sweet, *Gospel According to Starbucks,* 92.

4. Nanci Hellmich, *USA Today,* Nov. 9, 2009, www.usatoday.com /news/nation/census/2009-11-10-topblline10 _ST_N.htm.

5. Rieva Lesonsky, "Mobile Statistics Show Boomers Like E-Readers, Millenials [sic] Prefer Smartphones: Survey Says," *Huffington Post* blog, posted Aug. 29, 2011, www.huffingtonpost.com/2011 /08/29/mobile-statistics_n_940415.html.

6. See Sallkat Basu, "Visit these 5 (Virtual) Museums without Leaving Home," www.makeuseof.com/tag/visit-5-virtual-museums-leaving-home/.

7. John Roberto, "Faith Formation 2020: Envisioning Dynamic, Engaging, and Inspiring Faith Formation for the 21st Century," downloadable pdf, www.lifelongfaith.com/uploads/5/1/6/4/5164069 /umasce_consultation.pdf. See also the Faith Formation 2020 website, www.lifelongfaith.com/faith-formation-2020.html.

CHAPTER 15

1. J. Walker Smith and Ann Clurman, *Generation Ageless: How Baby Boomers Are Changing the Way We Live Today . . . and They're Just Getting Started* (New York: Collins Press, 2007), 150.

2. W. Barnes Tatum, *Jesus at the Movies* (Santa Rosa, CA: Polebridge Press), 2004.

3. Gregory Bassham and Eric Bronson, eds., *The Lord of the Rings and Philosophy* (Chicago: Open Court Press), 2003.

CHAPTER 16

1. Marc Freedman, *Encore: Finding Work that Matters in the Second Half of Life* (New York: Public Affairs, 2007), 19.

2. Phil Burgess, *Reboot: What to Do When Your Career Is Over but Your Life Isn't* (Victoria, BC, Canada: FriesenPress, 2011), 59–61.

3. Charles Arn, *Catch the Age Wave* (Kansas City: Beacon Hill Press, 1999), 69–70.

CHAPTER 17

1. Leonard Sweet, ed., *Communication and Change in American Religious History* (Grand Rapids: Eerdmans Press, 1993), 29.

2. Leonard Sweet, "Can the Mainstream Change Its Course?" in *Liberal Protestantism* (New York: Pilgrim Press, 1986), 248.

3. Elizabeth Jeffries, "Work Is Calling," in *Insights on Leadership* (New York: John Wiley and Sons, 1998), 29–30.

4. James C. Collins and Jerry I. Porras, *Built to Last* (New York: Harper Business, 1997), 77.

5. Sally and Robert Fitzgerald, eds., *Mystery and Manners* (New York: Farrar, Strauss and Giroux, 1970), 125.

RESOURCES

The suggestions I have outlined may or may not specifically fit the needs, size, or theology of your particular congregation; however, many ideas and methods can be effectively adapted to any ministry. They are intended to stimulate your interest in the topics raised in this book and encourage you to search for those tools that best promote ministry to Boomers in your congregation.

VISUALS USED BY PASS-A-GRILLE BEACH COMMUNITY CHURCH

Following are some visuals of some of the strategies/methods/techniques I have found to be effective, each of which has been described in a chapter of the book.

Chapter 12: "Publicity, Advertising, and Outreach"

Following are some of electronic billboards and coordinating yard signs used throughout the year in various Pass-a-Grille Beach Church ad campaigns.

Pass-a-Grille Beach Church's QR (quick response) code. Scanning this smartphone readable barcode gets you information about our church. Learn how to create one for your church at qrstuff.com /qr_stuff.html.

QR code

Chapter 13: "Seamless, Intimate, Experiential Worship"

Here is a sample of our worship bulletin. The inside (next page) shows our early (nontraditional) service on the left side and our later (traditional) service on the right side. The center allows room for notes, comments, or educational pieces pertaining to scripture.

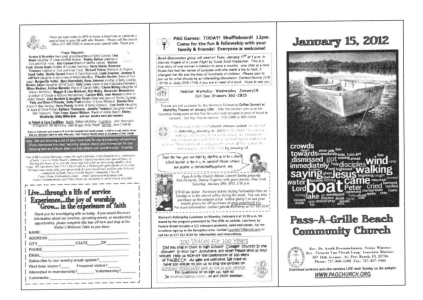

Outside of 11 x 17 trifold worship bulletin

Inside of 11 x 17 trifold worship bulletin

During Lent we erected this cross, made by a member, upon which worshipers attached prayer notes throughout the Lenten season.

On Pentecost, we not only hung red banners and streamers throughout the sanctuary, but also had in place this patio, propane-fed fire that burned throughout worship.

Chapter 14: "Artists of the Spirit"

Shown are two of the quilted seasonal altar cloths made for our sanctuary by a member who is an experienced quilter.

PRINT AND WEB RESOURCES

Discerning Spiritual Gifts and Life Plans

Brennfleck, Kevin and Kay. *Live Your Calling*. San Francisco: Jossey-Bass, 2005.

Episcopal Diocese of West Virginia. "A Spiritual Gifts Discernment Process." Downloadable pdf resource used by the Evangelical Lutheran and Episcopal Churches, which could be used by local congregations to implement discussion, www.wvdiocese.org /pages/pdfs /SpiritualGiftsDiscernment.pdf.

Kinghorn, Kenneth Cain. *Discovering Your Spiritual Gifts—A Personal Inventory Method*. Grand Rapids: Zondervan, 1981. Willow Creek Community Church in Barrington, Illinois, lists this resource.

Oswald, Roy M., and Otto Kroeger. *Personality Type and Religious Leadership*. Herndon, VA: The Alban Institute, 1988.

Rath, Tom. *Strengthsfinder2.0*. Based on the Clifton StrengthsFinder assessment, this book can assist with identifying personal strengths and concurrent areas for work or service. New York: Gallup Press, 2007.

Rees, Erik. *S.H.A.P.E.* Grand Rapids: Zondervan, 2008. This personal/ group study is based on the principles outlined in *The Purpose*

Driven Life by Rick Warren (Zondervan, 2006). Peter Wagner has a number of books on this subject.

Via Me! "All I Can Be." The free, twenty-four-point assessment available at www.viame.org can be used for general discussion or at least for an introduction to "a strengths-based life plan." For an additional $40, individuals can receive a more complete report with steps by which to create a map for their future. One $20 payment obtains a leader/interpreter guide.

Wagner, Peter. *Your Spiritual Gifts Can Help Your Church Grow.* Ventura, CA: Regal Books, 2005.

Small Group Programs and Discussion Materials

Agno, John G. *Books for Boomers.* Smashwords e-book edition, 2011.

Arn, Win and Charles. *Catch the Age Wave: A Handbook for Effective Ministry with Senior Adults.* Kansas City: Beacon Hill Press, 1999.

Buford, Bob. *Half Time—Changing Your Life Plan from Success to Significance.* Zondervan Groupware, videos series and study book. Grand Rapids: Zondervan, 2000.

Burgess, Phil. *ReBoot: What to Do When Your Career Is Over but Your Life Isn't.* Victoria, B.C.: Friesen Press, 2011.

Chittister, Joan. *The Gift of Years: Growing Older Gracefully.* New York: Blueridge, 2008.

Church, Forrest. *Life Craft: The Art of Meaning in the Everyday.* Boston: Beacon Press, 2000.

Dawson, Gerrit Scott, ed. *Companions in Christ: A Small-Group Experience in Spiritual Formation.* Nashville: Upper Room Books, 2001.

Hargrave, Terry. *Boomers on the Edge: Three Realities That Will Change Your Life Forever.* Grand Rapids: Zondervan, 2008.

Morgan, Richard I. *I Never Found That Rocking Chair: God's Call at Retirement.* Nashville: Upper Room Books, 1992.

Rohr, Richard. *Falling Upward: A Spirituality for the Two Halves of Life.* San Francisco: Jossey-Bass, 2011.

Health and Aging Discussion Materials

Astor, Bart. *Baby Boomer's Guide to Caring for Aging Parents.* Amazon: Kindle edition, 2011.

Church, Forrest. *Love and Death: My Journey through the Valley of the Shadow.* Boston: Beacon Press, 2008.

Gaughen, Shasta, ed. *Coping with Death: Contemporary Issues Study Guide.* Farmington Hills, MI: Greenhaven Press, 2003.

Soliz, Adela, ed. *Alzheimer's Disease: Contemporary Issues Study Guide.* Farmington Hills, MI: Greenhaven Press, 2003.

Swarts, Katherine. *The Aging Population. Opposing Viewpoints Series* (hardcover edition). Farmington Hills, MI: Greenhaven Press, 2009.

Fun Group-Building Ideas

Dockery, Karen. *Fun Friend-Making Activities for Adult Groups.* Loveland, CO: Vital Ministry, 1997.

Group Builders: High-Impact Ideas to Revolutionize Your Adult Ministry. Loveland, CO: Group Publishing, 2000.

Sipperly, Patrick. Fun Church Activities, 2/27/11, www.christian homechurch.com/1/post/2011/02/church-ideas-fun-church-activities.html.

Smith, Elizabeth. Fun Church Ideas, www.ehow.com/info_8507431 _fun-church-ideas.html.

Warnock, Chuck. 101 Outreach Ideas for Small Churches, chuck warnockblog.wordpress.com/2008/11/24/101-outreach-ideas-for-small-churches/.

Online Education/Discussion

Center for Progressive Renewal, www.progressiverenewal.org. Look for online learning and learning events.

Faith Formation 2020, www.LifelongFaith.com. This site offers John Roberto's extensive guide for ways to make your church a "Learning" congregation, including a downloadable working guide.

Scripture Echo, www.scriptureecho.com. Resources for worship and spiritual formation, including ways to pray.

The Thoughtful Christian online marketplace, www.thethoughtfulchristian.com/. This site offers books and downloadable Christian study resources, including studies that coincide with current movies.

Boomer-directed Websites (General Information and Volunteering Opportunities)

Boomer Café, www.boomercafe.com. Online magazine with general information about all things Baby Boomer.

Boomer Project, www.boomerproject.com. General Boomer information, particularly about marketing to this age group.

GoToRetirement, www.gotoretirement.com. A site offering financial guidance for Boomers.

Over 50 and Overseas, www.over50andoverseas.com; the UCC Volunteer Ministries page, www.ucc.org/volunteer/boomers.html; and World Volunteer Web, www.worldvolunteerweb.org. All offer international volunteer listings and opportunities.

The Senior Source, www.theseniorsource.org. This site of a greater Dallas, Texas, caregiving nonprofit agency has answers to many caregiver questions, appropriate for any location.

Church Websites Worth Examining

Crossroads Church, www.crossroads.net.

Highland Park United Methodist Church, www.hpumc.org.

Redeemer Presbyterian Church, www.redeemer.com.

Seacoast Church, www.seacoast.org.

Visual Swirl Design Resources, "60 of the Best Church Website Designs," www.visualswirl.com/inspiration/best-church-website-designs-2011/, posted by Chris Thurman on Jan. 12, 2012.

Worship and Media Apps, Aids, and Ideas

Creating Change: The Arts as Catalyst for Spiritual Transformation, Keri K. Wehlander, ed. Copper House B.C., 2007.

Experiential Worship, www.experientialworship.com, has participatory ideas for worship.

GloBible, www.globible.com, is a site with mobile applications that is visual and interactive.

Miller, Kim. *(Re)designing Worship.* Nashville: Abingdon Press, 2009.

Sing! Prayer and Praise. Cleveland: The Pilgrim Press, 2009.

The Work of the People, www.theworkofthepeople.com, offers visual and audio aids for mission and worship.

YouVersion, www.youversion.com, is a constantly expanding mobile resource for streaming sermon texts and educational pieces.

Business/Marketing Stuff

How to Use Facebook for Business, a free downloadable eBook, www.hubspot.com/marketing-ebook/how-to-use-facebook-to-grow-your-business/, will show ways to use Facebook for marketing your church.

Mancini, Will. "How to Develop a Compelling, Gospel-centered Tagline for Your Church,"www.willmancini.com/2011/02/how-to-develop-a-compelling-gospel-centered-tagline-for-your-church.html.

QR Stuff.com, www.qrstuff.com/qr_stuff.html, helps you generate a QR code.

BIBLIOGRAPHY

"10 Ways Boomers Will Transform 2012," Boomer Project, *Jumpin' Jack Flash,* January 4, 2012, www.boomerproject.com/documents/jumpin_jack/2012_january.php.

AARP, "Top 10 Baby Boomer Myths: Separating Fiction from Myth." March 6, 2012, www.babyboomer-magazine.com/news/165/ARTICLE/1298/2010-04-01.html.

ABC News. "Inheritance and Wealth Transfer to Baby Boomers," December 27, 2011.

Allyn, Bobby. "More Parents Helping Adult Children Get Homes, Cars," *USA Today,* February 2, 2012.

Amick, Jeremy. "Four Ways to Make Passion Their Reason for Serving," *Church Volunteer Central,* January 24, 2012.

Anderson, Kerby. "Baby Boomerangs," Leadership U, September 6, 2011, www.leaderu.com/orgs/probe/docs/boomer.html.

Arn, Charles, and Win Arn. *Catch the Age Wave: A Handbook for Effective Ministry with Senior Adults.* Boston: Beacon Hill Press, 1999.

"Baby Boomer Facts," Get Involved! National and Community Service. August 27, 2011, www.getinvolved.gov/newsroom/programs/factsheet _boomers.asp.

Barrick, Audrey. "Churches Recognize Large, Underutilized Baby Boomers," *CP Church & Ministries,* September 12, 2011, www.christianpost.com/news/churches-recognize-large-underutilized-baby-boomers-26448/.

Bassham, Gregory, and Eric Bronson. *The Lord of the Rings and Philosophy: One Book to Rule them All.* Chicago: Open Court Press, 2003.

Boomer Cafe, "Tom Brokaw Looks at Baby Boomers," August 18, 2011, www.boomercafe.com/2010/03/03/tom-brokaw-looks-at-baby-boomers/.

Brennfleck, Kevin, and Kay Marie Brennfleck. *Live Your Calling: A Practical Guide to Finding and Fulfilling Your Mission in Life.* San Francisco: Jossey-Bass, 2005.

Buford, Bob. *Half Time: Winning Strategies for the Second Half of Your Life.* Grand Rapids: Zondervan, 1998.

———. *Finish Well: What People Who Really Live Do Differently.* Nashville: Thomas Nelson, 2005.

Burgess, Phillip. *Reboot! What to Do When Your Career Is Over but Your Life Isn't.* Victoria, BC: Friesen Press, 2011.

Chittister, Joan. *The Gift of Years: Growing Older Gracefully.* New York: Blueridge, 2010.

Cohn, D'Vera, and Paul Taylor. "Baby Boomers Approach 65— Glumly." Pew Research Center, Pew Social and Demographic Trends, December 20, 2010, www.pewsocialtrends.org/2010/12/20/baby-boomers-approach-65-glumly/.

Collins, Jim. C., and Jerry I. Porras. *Built to Last: Successful Habits of Visionary Companies.* New York: HarperBusiness, 2004.

Crary, David. "Boomers Will Be Pumping Billions into the Anti-Aging Industry." *Huffington Post,* August 8, 2011, www.huffingtonpost.com/2011/08/20/boomers-anti-aging-industry_n_932109.html.

Cravit, David. *The New Old: How the Boomers Are Changing Everything . . . Again.* Toronto: ECW Press, 2008.

Dell, Kristina. "Financial Woes Force Boomers to Work Longer. That's Good." *Time Business,* November, 18, 2008, www.time.com/time/business/article/0,8599,1860323,00.html.

Dockry, Karen. *Fun Friend-Making Activities for Adult Groups.* Loveland: Group Publishing, 1997.

Dunham & Company. "New Study Shows Online Giving Is Important to Donors 60+." December 6, 2011, dunhamandcompany.com/2011/12/new-study-shows-online-giving-is-important-to-donors-60/.

Dychtwald, Ken, and Daniel Kadlec. *A New Purpose: Redefining Money, Family, Work, Retirement, and Success.* New York: Harper Press, 2010.

Engaging Worship: 20 Blueprints for Experiential Church Services. Loveland: Group Publishing, 2009.

Focalyst. "Boomers 'Not-So-Me Generation—Apt to Volunteer Time, Shop Green." Marketing Charts, September 22, 2008, www

.mediabuyerplanner.com/entry/33461/boomers-not-so-me-generation-apt-to-volunteer-time-shop-green/.

Freedman, Marc. *Prime Time: How Baby Boomers Will Revolutionize Retirement and Transform America.* New York: Public Affairs, 2002.

———. *Encore: Finding Work That Matters in the Second Half of Life.* New York: PublicAffairs, 2007.

Freedman, Samuel G. "Congregations Reeling from Decline in Donations." *The New York Times,* September 24, 2010, www.nytimes.com/2010/09/25/us/25religion.html?_r=1.

Fritz, Joanne. "Tapping the Volunteer Power of Baby Boomers." About.com, Non-profit Charitable Orgs, nonprofit.about.com/od/volunteers/a/boomervolunteer.htm.

Gallagher, David P. *Senior Adult Ministry in the 21st Century: Step-by-Step Strategies for Reaching People over 50.* Eugene: Wipf & Stock, 2006.

Gentzler, Richard H. Jr. *Aging and Ministry in the 21st Century: An Inquiry Approach.* Nashville: Discipleship Resources, 2008.

"Giving." *The Presbyterian Outlook,* December 15, 2011.

Green, Brent. *Marketing to Leading-Edge Baby Boomers: Perceptions, Principles, Practices & Predictions.* Ithaca: Paramount Market Publishing, 2006.

Group Builders: 50 High-Impact Ideas to Revolutionize Your Adult Ministry. Loveland: Group Publishing, 2000.

Hanson, Amy. *Baby Boomers and Beyond: Tapping the Ministry Talents and Passions of Adults over 50.* San Francisco: Jossey-Bass, 2010.

Hauerwas, Stanley, ed. *Growing Old in Christ.* Grand Rapids: Eerdmans, 2003.

Haywood, Michael Anne. "A Spiritual Gifts Discernment Process." http://home.earthlink.net/~haywoodm/SpiritualGiftsDiscernment.html.

Hicks, Rick, and Kathy Hicks. *Boomers, Xers, and Other Strangers: Understanding Generational Differences That Divide Us.* Carol Stream, IL: Tyndale House, 1999.

Houston, J. M., and M. A. Parker. *Vision for the Aging Church: Renewing Ministry for and by Seniors.* Downers Grove, IL: IVP Academic, 2011.

IHRSA. "Global Health Club Industry Surpasses 128 Million Members." Success by Association, May 26, 2011, www.ihrsa.org /media-center/2011/5/26/global-health-club-industry-surpasses-128-million-members-th.html.

Isaacson, Walter. *Steve Jobs*. New York: Simon and Schuster, 2011.

Jeffries, Elizabeth. "Work Is Calling." In *Insights on Leadership: Service, Stewardship, Spirit, and Servant Leadership*. New York: John Wiley and Sons, 1997.

Jones, Landon Y. *Great Expectations—America & the Baby Boom Generation*. New York: BookSurge, 2008.

Kushner, Harold. *Who Needs God?* New York: Fireside, 2002.

Lesonsky, Rieva. "Mobile Statistics Show Boomers Like E-Readers, Millenials [sic] Prefer Smartphones: Survey Says," *Huffington Post* blog, posted August 29, 2011, www.huffingtonpost.com /2011/08/29/mobile-statistics_n_940415.html.

Light, Paul C. *Baby Boomers*. New York: W.W. Norton, 1988.

Litsky, Frank. "Cowher Resigns, Stops Short of Retiring." *The New York Times,* January 6, 2007, www.nytimes.com/2007/01/06 /sports/football/06cowher.html.

Love, Jeffrey. "Political Behavior and Values across the Generations: A Summary of Selected Findings." *AARP*, July, 2004.

McIntosh, Gary. *One Church, Four Generations: Understanding and Reaching All Ages in Your Church*. Grand Rapids: Baker Books, 2002.

———. "Perspectives and Practices for Ministry with Baby Boomers." In *Lifelong Faith*. Vol. 4.4 (Winter 2010), www.lifelong faith.com/uploads/5/1/6/4/5164069/lifelong_faith_journal_4.4.pdf.

Miller, Kim. *(Re)designing Worship: Creating Powerful God Experiences*. Nashville: Abingdon Press, 2009.

Mitchell, Heidi. "A Whole Other Ball Game." *The Wall Street Journal,* January 28, 2012, online.wsj.com/article/SB10001424052 9702046165045771729627336477798.html.

Morais, Richard C. "The Age of Charity-Clicks." Barrons: *Penta,* December 22, 2011, blogs.barrons.com/penta/2011/12/22/the-age-of-charity-clicks/.

Morgan, Richard, ed. *Dimensions of Older Adult Ministry: A Handbook*. Louisville: Witherspoon Press, 2006.

New York Life. "Boomers' Inheritance: The Sobering Reality." May 10, 2012, www.newyorklife.com/nyl/v/index.jsp?contentId=13385 &vgnextoid=f576e62f139d2210a2b3019d221024301cacRCRD.

O'Connor, Flannery. *Mystery and Manners: Occasional Prose.* New York: Farrar, Strauss and Giroux, 1970.

Oswald, Roy, and Otto Kroeger. *Personality Type and Religious Leadership.* Washington, D.C.: Alban Institute, 1988.

Pennington, Bill. "Baby Boomers Stay Active and So Do Their Doctors." *The New York Times,* April 16, 2006, www.nytimes .com/2006/04/16/sports/16boomers.html?_r=1&pagewanted=all.

Perrault, Mike, and Keith Matheny. "As Golf Declines, Life on the Links Ain't What It Used to Be," in *USA Today,* January 16, 2012, www.usatoday.com/money/economy/housing/story/2012-01-15/golf-communities-real-estate/52591988/1.

Pew Research Center. "The Generation Gap and the 2012 Election: Angry Silents, Disengaged Millennials." Pew Research Center Publications, November 3, 2011, www.people-press.org/2011 /11/03/the-generation-gap-and-the-2012-election-3/.

Phipps, Jennie L. "Boomers Calling It Quits by 65," in *Retirement Blog,* April 4, 2012, www.bankrate.com/financing/retirement/boomers -calling-it-quits-by-65/.

Piegza, Edward. "New Survey Shows Baby Boomers Seeking Active Adventure Travel." Classic Journeys, January 21, 2012, www .classicjourneys.com/blog/new/surveys-show-baby-boomers-seeking-active-adventure-travel/.

Powell, Robert. "Many of Us Won't Be Able to Retire until Our 80s." Market Watch. *The Wall Street Journal,* June 9, 2011, articles .marketwatch.com/2011-06-09/finance/30766873_1_retirement-income-adequacy-aarp-report-employee-benefit-research-institute.

Rath, Tom. "Strengthsfinder 2.0." New York: Gallup Press, 2007.

Rees, Erik. *S.H.A.P.E.: Finding and Fulfilling Your Unique Purpose for Life.* Grand Rapids: Zondervan, 2006.

Reichenal, Wendy. "Boomers Look toward an Older Generation's Icon," April 28, 2011, www.boomercafe.com/2011/04/28/boomer -look-toward-an-older-generations-icon/.

Roberto, John. "Developing Faith Formation for the Baby Boom Generation." *Lifelong Faith.* Vol.4.4 (Winter 2010), www.lifelong faith.com/uploads/5/1/6/4/5164069/lifelong_faith_journal _4.4.pdf.

Rognlien, Bob. *Experiential Worship: Encountering God with Heart, Soul, Mind and Strength (Quiet Times for the Heart).* Colorado Springs: Navpress, 2004.

Roof, Wade C. *Spiritual Marketplace: Baby Boomers and the Remaking of American Religion.* Princeton, NJ: Princeton University Press, 2001.

Saltus, Richard. "Losing Touch Reviving the Dying Art of Hands-on Medicine," *The Boston Globe,* June 7, 1999, www.highbeam .com/doc/1P2-8546764.html.

Scanlon, Leslie. "Expert Says Churches Must Adapt to New Profile in Giving." *The Presbyterian Outlook,* November 12, 2011, www .pres-outlook.com/reports-a-resources3/presbyterian-heritage -articles3/11964-expert-says-churches-must-adapt-to-new -profile-of-charitable-giving.html.

Schuller, Robert H. *Your Church Has a Fantastic Future: Fresh Possibilities for Church Growth.* Ventura: Regal Books, 1986.

Simmons, Henry, and June Wilson. *Soulful Again: Ministry through the Stages of Adulthood.* Macon, GA: Smyth and Helwys, 2001.

Slatalla, Michelle. "Five Fascinating Philanthropists." *Barrons,* December 5, 2011, online.barrons.com/article/SB50001424052748704854004577052601132573024.html#articleTabs_article%3D1.

Smith, J. Walker, and Ann Clurman. *Generation Ageless: How Baby Boomers Are Changing the Way We Live Today . . . and They're Just Getting Started.* New York: Collins Business, 2007.

Steinhorn, Leonard. *The Greater Generation (In Defense of the Baby Boom Legacy).* New York: St. Martin's Press, 2006.

Sullivan, Julie. "Baby Boomers, who drove the cultural shift to SUVs and consumerism, now driving the shift to public transit and yoga." *Oregon Live,* May 10, 2011, www.Oregonlive.com/health /index.ssf/2011/05/baby_boomers_drive_the_cultura.html.

Sweet, Leonard. "Can the Mainstream Change Its Course?" In *Liberal Protestantism Realities and Possibilities.* New York: Pilgrim Press, 1986.

Sweet, Leonard, ed. *Communication and Change in American Religious History*. Grand Rapids: Eerdmans, 1993.

Sweet, Leonard. *The Gospel According to Starbucks: Living with a Grande Passion*. Colorado Springs: WaterBrook Press, 2007.

Tatum, W. Barnes. *Jesus at the Movies: A Guide to the First Hundred Years*. Santa Rosa, CA: Polebridge Press, 2004.

Taylor, Paul. "Baby Boomers Approach Age 60: From the Age of Aquarius to the Age of Responsibility." Pew Research Center, "A Social Trends Report," December 8, 2005, pewresearch.org /assets/social/pdf/socialtrends-boomers120805.pdf.

Thibault, Jane M. *10 Gospel Promises for Later Life*. Nashville: Upper Room Books, 2006.

Twain, Mark. *Life on the Mississippi*. Salt Lake City: Project Gutenberg Ebooks, 2006, www.gutenberg.org/files/245/245-h/245-h.htm.

Visual Swirl Design Resources. "60 of the Best Church Website Designs." www.visualswirl.com/inspiration/best-church-website-designs-2011/, posted by Chris Thurman on Jan. 12, 2012.

Warren, Rick. *The Purpose Driven Life: What on Earth Am I Here For?* Grand Rapids: Zondervan, 2002.

Wehlander, Keri, ed. *Creating Change—the Arts as Catalyst for Spiritual Transformation*. Kelowna: Copper House, 2008.

Wilhem, Mark, Patrick Rooney, and Eugene Tempel. "Changes in Religious Giving Reflect Changes in Involvement." The Center on Philanthropy. Indiana University, Indiana University-Purdue University, Indianapolis, 2007.

Yohn, Rick. *Discover Your Spiritual Gift and Use It*. Clovis: Heritage Builders, 2011.

Zickuhr, Kathryn. "Major Trends in Online Activities." Pew Internet & American Life Project. December 16, 2010, pewinternet.org /Reports/2010/Generations-2010/Trends.aspx?view=all.